Branding and Brand Equity

KEVIN LANE KELLER

MARKETING SCIENCE INSTITUTE

Cambridge, Massachusetts

Copyright © 2002 Kevin Lane Keller
Published by Marketing Science Institute
1000 Massachusetts Ave.
Cambridge, MA 02138
Design by Joyce C. Weston
Printed in the United States of America
ISBN 0-9657114-2-0

Contents

About the Series

The Relevant Knowledge Series, published by the Marketing Science Institute, is intended to fill a gap in the market. Put simply, there has been no "home" for high quality, detailed, and comprehensible work on focused topics whose length is greater than a working paper or journal article and less than a full-scale textbook or tradebook.

Each monograph in the series will summarize and "translate" state-of-the-art knowledge on important and well-researched topics. The MSI research priorities, established every two years, offer a starting point for such an endeavor. Thus, monograph titles will reflect longstanding priority topics: promotion, branding, new products, and marketing metrics, among others.

Monographs in the series will be of several types. Some will define a topic, summarize extant research, and discuss measurement issues and metrics as well as managerial implications and directions for future research. Other "method-based" monographs will describe and demystify methodologies, compare simple alternatives, and discuss relevant uses. Still others will gather papers on a single topic, with an integrating summary and directions for future research.

Branding and Brand Equity represents the second book in this series; it follows *Sales Promotion* by Scott Neslin. Here, Kevin Keller provides valuable insights into the role of brands and brand management by summarizing the extensive research in this area. Given the importance of brands, *Branding and Brand Equity* should prove to be informative and interesting to a broad range of readers.

Donald R. Lehmann
Columbia University
MSI Executive Director 2001–03

ACKNOWLEDGEMENTS

A version of this monograph appears in *Handbook of Marketing,* edited by Robin Wensley and Barton Weitz, published by Sage Publications. Appreciation is extended to Susan Fournier and Deborah Roedder John for constructive comments and suggestions.

Kevin Lane Keller
Dartmouth College

Executive Summary

Branding has become a top management priority for a broad cross-section of organizations in recent years. Many firms have come to realize that one of their most valuable assets is the intangible asset that is their brands. As a consequence, branding principles have been applied in virtually every setting: with physical goods, services, retail stores, people, organizations, places, and even ideas. Driven in part by this intense industry interest, academic researchers and marketing commentators have explored a number of different brand-related topics in recent years, generating hundreds of papers, articles, research reports, and books on branding.

This monograph highlights what has been learned in recent years, from an academic perspective, in the study of branding and brand equity. Academic research provides insight into a number of issues in building, measuring, and managing brand equity, as follows.

Branding Fundamentals

Academic researchers generally agree that "branding" is all about creating differences and endowing products and services with the "power" of brand equity. Although specific views of brand equity differ, academic observers are largely in agreement that brand equity should be defined in terms of marketing effects uniquely attributable to a brand. In other words, brand equity exists when customers react more favorably to a product and the way it is marketed when the brand is identified, as compared to when it is not.

Most marketing academics also agree with the following basic principles of branding and brand equity: (1) differences in outcomes from current marketing activities arise from the "added value" endowed to a product as a result of past marketing activity for the brand; (2) this value can be created for a brand in many different ways; (3) brand equity provides a common denominator for interpreting marketing strategies and assessing the value of a brand; and (4) the value of a brand can be manifested or exploited in many different ways to benefit the firm.

In terms of this last point, academic research shows that the benefits to creating a strong brand with equity include:

- Improved perceptions of product performance

- Greater loyalty

- Less vulnerability to competitive marketing actions and marketing crises

- Larger margins

- More inelastic consumer response to price increases and more elastic consumer response to price decreases

- Greater trade cooperation and support

- Increased marketing communication effectiveness

- Licensing opportunities and additional brand extension opportunities

Conceptualizing Brand Equity

Three main streams of academic research have formally defined or conceptualized brand equity, based on consumer psychology, economics, or biology and sociology.

Researchers studying branding effects from a consumer psychology perspective adopt concepts and principles from cognitive psychology, social psychology, and social cognition to develop models of brand equity and of how consumers make brand-related decisions. For example, associative network memory models view the brand as a node in memory linked to many different associations.

Other researchers take an information-economics perspective on the value (or equity) consumers ascribe to brands. According to this view, when consumers are uncertain about product attributes, brands can inform consumers about product positions and signal that their product claims are credible. By reducing consumer uncertainty, brands thus lower information costs and the risk perceived by consumers.

Finally, some researchers have studied branding from a sociological, anthropological, or biological perspective, considering the broader cultural meaning of brands and products, or from a perceptual or biological perspective, applying subconscious theories and concepts to branding effects.

All three theoretical approaches to branding, to some extent, share the strengths and weaknesses of the disciplines in which they are rooted. Like other areas of marketing, however, adopting, or at least recognizing, the advantages of these multiple perspectives may offer deeper and richer understanding of branding and brand equity.

Brand Building

Research has also examined how brands can be built. Some research concentrates on the brand itself, for example, the brand name or logo, and shows that these elements can clearly contribute to brand equity by helping to convey product meaning. These effects can be quite context dependent (e.g., depending on the cultural setting) and brand elements must be carefully designed.

Academic research also provides theoretical and empirical insights into brand "intangibles," exploring concepts such as brand personality, experiences, relationships, and communities. This research shows how brand intangibles help make a brand more meaningful and relevant to consumers, creating stronger brand ties as a result. At a corporate brand level, research also shows that corporate brands can have a broad set of associations that can facilitate product acceptance.

Research on Brand Extensions

The most heavily researched area in branding is brand extensions. A synthesis of these studies yields the following general principles and findings:

Parent Brand/Extension Fit

- Successful brand extensions occur when the parent brand is seen as having favorable associations and there is a perception of fit between the parent brand and the extension product.

- The bases of fit include product-related attributes and benefits as well as non-product-related attributes and benefits related to common usage situations or user types.

- Concrete attribute associations tend to be more difficult to extend than abstract benefit associations. In addition, consumers may transfer associations that are positive in the original product class but become negative in the extension context. Consumers may infer negative associations about an extension, perhaps even based on other inferred positive associations.

- Depending on consumer knowledge of the categories, perceptions of fit may be based on technical or manufacturing commonalities or more surface considerations such as necessary or situational complementarity (e.g., products used together in the same consumption setting).

- The most effective advertising strategy for an extension is one which emphasizes information about the extension (rather than reminders about the parent brand).

Types of Extensions

- High quality brands "stretch" farther than average quality brands and can be successfully extended into more dissimilar product categories, although both types of brands have boundaries and limits as to where they can extend.

- A brand that is seen as prototypical of a product category can be difficult to extend outside the category.

- It can be difficult to extend into a product class that is seen as easy-to-make.

- Vertical (specifically, downward) extensions can be difficult and often require sub-branding strategies.

Extension Feedback Effects

- A successful extension not only contributes to the parent brand image but also enables a brand to be extended even farther.

- An unsuccessful extension hurts the parent brand only when there is a strong basis of fit between the two.

- An unsuccessful extension in a dissimilar product category does not prevent a firm from "backtracking" and introducing a more similar extension.

Brand Strategies and Alliances

Finally, research has explored brand strategies and alliances, and how different combinations of brand names—those belonging to the company or to other companies—impact consumer response and can improve product evaluations. Research shows that sub-branding, that is, combining a corporate or family brand name with individual brand names, can enhance extension evaluations, especially if the extension is more removed from the original product category and less similar in fit. Moreover, a sub-brand can also protect the parent brand from any negative feedback.

The order and prominence of the brand name components will moderate these effects and influence the flow of equity. Similarly, strategically chosen brand alliances with brands from other categories and companies have also been shown to improve consumer brand evaluations.

Introduction

Although brand management has been an important activity for some companies for decades, branding has only emerged as a top management priority for a broad cross-section of organizations since the mid-1980s. A number of factors have contributed to this trend, but perhaps the most important is the growing realization that one of the firms' most valuable assets is an intangible one: their brands. As a consequence, branding principles have been applied in virtually every setting where consumer choice of some kind is involved: with physical goods, services, retail stores, people, organizations, places, or ideas. Driven in part by this intense industry interest, academic researchers and marketing commentators have explored a number of brand-related topics in recent years, generating hundreds of papers, articles, research reports, and books on branding.[1]

The purpose of this monograph is to review and provide some context for, and interpretation of, this research. The goal is to highlight what has been learned, from an academic perspective, in the study of branding and brand equity, as well as what gaps still exist. Although emphasis is placed on research published since 1990, earlier "classics" or noteworthy studies are highlighted where appropriate.[2] I concentrate primarily on those important issues in building, measuring, and managing brand equity that have received at least some academic attention. Consequently, I do not cover in detail such issues as brand recovery, revitalization of classic or heritage brands, brand architecture design, and brand stewardship—topics that have been discussed in a number of trade books and publications.

I begin by reviewing the fundamentals of branding and brand equity measurement. Next, I discuss factors affecting the choice and design of brand elements such as brand names and logos, as well as some legal issues related to branding. Third, I consider brand "intangibles"—the means by which a brand "transcends" its product functionality. I also review research concerning brand personality, experiences, relationships, and communities as well as corporate images. Fourth, I review a number of issues with respect to brand extensions—the most widely studied area of branding—and examine moderating and mediating factors and managerial issues in detail. Fifth, I examine brand strategies and brand alliances and the means by which brands leverage their brand equity, as well as borrow brand equity from others. I conclude by offering some summary observations and identifying research priorities in branding and brand management.

Kevin Lane Keller

Branding and Brand Equity

Branding Fundamentals

According to the American Marketing Association, a brand is "a name, term, sign, symbol, or combination of them that is designed to identify the goods or services of one seller or group of sellers and to differentiate them from those of competitors." Technically speaking, whenever a marketer creates a new name, logo, or symbol for a new product, he or she has created a brand. However, many practicing managers define a brand as creating a certain amount of awareness, reputation, and prominence in the marketplace. Thus, a distinction can be made between the AMA definition of a "small b" brand and the industry viewpoint of a "big B" Brand. It is important to recognize this distinction; disagreements about branding principles or guidelines often revolve around the definition of a "brand." With this caveat, we turn to the topics of brand effects and functions, conceptualizing branding, and measuring brand equity.

Brand Effects and Functions

A number of studies have explored the effects of brands on consumer behavior and the effectiveness of marketing programs (see Hoeffler and Keller [2001] for a comprehensive review, as well as Yoo, Donthu, and Lee [2000] for some empirical tests). In these studies, "brand type" or some such variable is included in the research design, either directly as an independent variable or indirectly as a moderator variable interacting with one or more independent variables. In either case, research reveals numerous positive effects and advantages from creating a "strong" brand, where brand strength may reflect macro brand considerations such as market leadership or market share position as well as micro brand considerations such as consumer familiarity, knowledge, preferences, or loyalty. Findings from these studies include the following.

Product-related Effects   Brand name has been shown to be positively associated with consumer product evaluations, perceptions of quality, and purchase rates (Brown and Dacin 1997; Day and Deutscher 1982; Dodds, Monroe, and Grewal 1991; Leclerc, Schmitt, and Dubé 1994; Rao and Monroe 1989). This is especially apparent with difficult-to-assess "experience" goods (Wernerfelt 1988) and as the uniqueness of brand associations increases (Feinberg, Kahn, and McAlister 1992). In addition, familiarity with a brand is shown to increase consumer confidence, attitude toward the brand, and purchase intention (Laroche, Kim, and Zhou 1996; Feinberg, Kahn, and McAlister 1992) and to mitigate the potential impact of a negative trial experience (Smith 1993). Chaudhuri and Holbrook (2001) show that brand trust and brand affect combine to determine purchase loyalty and attitudinal loyalty; in turn, purchase loyalty leads to greater market share and attitudinal loyalty leads to higher relative price for the brand. Such effects have contributed to long-term category leadership for some brands. However, in an unbiased sample of 100 categories over a 76-year period, Golder (2000) finds that many leading brands have lost their leadership. Tellis and Golder (1996) identify five key factors for enduring market leadership: vision of the market, managerial persistence, financial commitment, relentless innovation, and asset leverage.

Price-related Effects   Several studies demonstrate that brand leaders can command higher prices (Simon 1979; Agrawal 1996; Park and Srinivasan 1994; Sethuraman 1996) and are more immune to price increases (Bucklin, Gupta, and Han 1995; Sivakumar and Raj 1997). In addition, brand leaders draw a disproportionate amount of share from smaller share competitors (Allenby and Rossi 1991; Grover and Srinivasan 1992; Russell and Kamakura 1994). At the same time, prior research demonstrates that market leaders are relatively immune to price competition from these small share brands (Bemmaor and Mouchoux 1991; Blattberg and Wisniewski 1989; Bucklin, Gupta, and Han 1995; Sivakumar and Raj 1997). Finally, lower levels of price sensitivity are found for households that are more loyal (Krishnamurthi and Raj 1991). Advertising may play a role in the decreases in price sensitivity (Kanetkar, Weinberg, and Weiss 1992). Boulding, Lee, and Staelin (1994) find that unique advertising messages (e.g., product differentiation for high quality products and low price messages for low price leaders) lead to a reduction in susceptibility to future price competition.

Communication-related Effects   A number of communication effects have been attributed to well-known and liked brands (Sawyer 1981). Brown and Stayman (1992) maintain that "halo effects" related to the positive feelings toward a brand can positively bias the evaluation of brand advertising. Humor in ads seems to be more effective for familiar or already favorably evaluated brands than for unfamiliar or less favorably evaluated brands (Chattopadhyay and Basu 1990; Stewart and Furse 1986; Weinburger and Gulas 1992). Similarly, with comparative ads (Belch 1981), the nature of the brand seems to affect the degree of negativity in the consumer's reaction (see also Kamins and Marks 1991). Consumers are more likely to have a negative reaction to ad repetition with unknown as opposed to strong brands (Calder and Sternthal 1980; Campbell and Keller 2002). Familiar brands appear to better withstand competitive ad interference (Kent and Allen 1994). Van Osselaer and Alba (2000) show that when consumers learn the brand name-product quality relationship prior to the product attributes-quality relationship, they were less attentive to the product attributes-quality relationship.

In addition, panel diary members who are highly loyal to a brand increase purchases when advertising for the brand increases (Raj 1982). Other advantages associated with more advertising include increased likelihood of being the focus of attention (Dhar and Simonson 1992; Simonson, Huber, and Payne 1988) and increased "brand interest" (Machleit, Allen, and Madden 1993). Ahluwalia, Burnkrant, and Unnava (2000) demonstrate that consumers who have a high level of commitment to a brand are more likely to counter-argue with negative information (see also Laczniak, DeCarlo, and Ramaswami 2001). This may be why strong brands are shown to be better able to weather a product-harm crisis (Dawar and Pillutla 2000).

Channel-related Effects   Montgomery (1975) finds that products from the top firms in an industry have a much higher chance of being accepted in the channel and gaining shelf space in supermarkets. Research also suggests that stores are more likely to feature well-known brands if they are trying to convey a high quality image (Lal and Narasimhan 1996).

In short, across a wide range of marketing activities, there are demonstrable advantages from creating a strong brand.

Conceptualizing Brand Equity

As with advertising and other marketing phenomena, a number of different theoretical mechanisms and perspectives have been brought to bear in the study of branding. Three main streams of academic research have formally defined or conceptualized brand equity: consumer psychology, economics, and biology and sociology.

Psychology-based Approaches Researchers studying branding effects from a cognitive psychology perspective frequently adopt associative network memory models to develop theories and hypotheses, in part because of the comprehensiveness and diagnostic value they offer (see Krishnan [1996] and Henderson, Iacobucci, and Calder [1998] for empirical demonstrations, as well as Lassar, Mittal, and Sharma [1995]). Using this approach, the brand is seen as a node in memory linked with different associations of varying strengths. Relatedly, prior research (e.g., Boush and Loken 1991) suggests that consumers see brands as categories that, over time, are associated with specific attributes, based in part on the attributes associated with products that represent individual members of the brand category (Loken and John 1993).

Researchers also rely on concepts and principles from social psychology and social cognition in developing models of consumer brand-related decisions, for example, affect referral mechanisms, attributional processes, accessibility-diagnosticity considerations, expectancy-value formulations, and so on. Researchers also use models of consumer inference-making fairly extensively. Teas and Grapentine (1996) construct a framework of the role of brand names in consumer purchase decision-making processes from a marketing research perspective that highlights some of these considerations.

Two well-established models of brand equity that rely on consumer psychology principles merit further discussion (see also Farquhar 1989).

In three books and numerous papers, Aaker (1991, 1996; Aaker and Joachimsthaler 2000) approaches brand equity from a managerial and corporate strategy perspective but with a consumer behavior underpinning. He defines brand equity as a set of four categories of brand assets (or liabilities) linked to a brand's name or symbol that add to (or subtract from) the value provided by a product or service to a firm and/or to that firm's customers: brand awareness, perceived quality, brand associations, and brand loyalty. Aaker develops a number of distinct and useful concepts related to brand identity, brand architecture, and brand marketing programs and addresses a number of managerial branding challenges (Aaker 1994; Aaker and Joachimsthaler 1999; Joachimsthaler and Aaker 1997).

Keller (1993, 1998) approaches brand equity primarily from a consumer behavior perspective. He defines "customer-based brand equity" as the differential effect that brand knowledge has on consumer or customer response to the marketing of that brand. According to this model, a brand is said to have positive customer-based brand equity when customers react more favorably to a product and the way it is marketed when the brand is identified, as compared to when it is not (e.g., when a fictitiously named or unnamed version of the product is used). Customer-based brand equity exists when the consumer has a high level of awareness and familiarity with the brand and holds some strong, favorable, and unique brand associations in memory. Keller views brand building as a series of steps: establishing the proper brand identity, creating the appropriate brand meaning, eliciting the right brand responses, and forging appropriate brand relationships with customers (Keller 2001). Achieving these four steps, according to his model, involves establishing six core brand values: brand salience, brand performance, brand imagery, brand judgments, brand feelings, and brand resonance. He also develops a number of different related concepts and considers a number of different managerial applications (Keller 1999a, b, 2000).

The Aaker and Keller models have much in common with each other, as well as with other psychologically based approaches to brand equity. Most importantly, both acknowledge that brand equity represents the "added value" endowed to a product as a result, in part, of past investments in marketing for the brand. It should be noted that the Aaker and

Keller models rely to some extent on spreading activation processes from an associative network model of memory whereby the ease of recalling favorable brand associations is a prime determinant of brand equity. Janiszewski and van Osselaer (2000) offer some evidence to suggest that a "connectionist" model of brand-quality association may provide a more robust explanation of consumer reactions to various branding strategies under certain conditions (see also van Osselaer and Janiszewski 2001). According to their model, consumers are assumed to be adaptive learners who are "learning to value"; the spreading activation perspective, Janiszewski and van Osselaer argue, is more relevant for consumers who are "learning to recall." In this regard, Meyers-Levy (1989) shows that a large number of associations is not necessarily advantageous and could produce interference effects and lower memory performance.

Economics-based Approaches Although behavioral models provide the dominant basis for studying branding effects and brand equity, other valuable viewpoints have also emerged. Erdem (1998a, b) takes an information-economics perspective on the value (or equity) ascribed to brands by consumers (see also Sappington and Wernerfelt 1985; Wernerfelt 1988; Montgomery and Wernerfelt 1992). Based in part on a premise of the imperfect and asymmetrical information structure of markets, Erdem's approach centers on the role of credibility as the primary determinant of what she terms "consumer-based brand equity." When consumers are uncertain about product attributes, according to Erdem, firms may use brands to inform consumers about product positions and to signal that their product claims are credible. By reducing consumer uncertainty, brands are seen as lowering information costs and the risk perceived by consumers. She provides empirical support for these signaling mechanisms in an umbrella branding application to the oral hygiene market.

Relatedly, Rao, Qu, and Ruekert (1999) argue that a brand name can credibly convey unobservable quality when false claims would result in intolerable economic losses, due to losses of reputation or sunk investments or losses of future profits. In a brand alliance application with hypothetical television brands, they show that consumers' evaluations of the quality of a product with an important unobservable attribute are enhanced when the brand is allied with a second brand that is perceived to be vulnerable to consumer sanctions.

Sociology- and Biology-based Approaches   Other branding research is based on sociological, anthropological, or biological perspectives. For example, McCracken (1986, 1993) considers the broader cultural meaning of brands and products (see also Richins 1994). As outlined in subsequent sections, other researchers explore topics such as brand communities (Schouten and McAlexander 1995; Muniz and O'Guinn 2001; Solomon and Englis 1992) and brand relationships (Fournier 1998). (See Ratneshwar, Mick, and Huffman [2000] for some recent commentary.)

Other researchers approach branding by examining consumer perception—and even consumer subconscious. For example, as described in more detail below, Schmitt (1999a, b) views branding experientially in terms of its effects on all five senses. Zaltman (Zaltman and Higie 1993; Zaltman and Coulter 1995) use metaphors as a guiding theme and qualitative research techniques to uncover the mental models driving consumer behavior with respect to brands.

To some extent, all three theoretical approaches share the strengths and weaknesses of their respective disciplines. Like other areas of marketing, however, adopting, or at least recognizing the advantages of, multiple perspectives can potentially offer a deeper and richer understanding of branding and brand equity.

Counter-arguments to the Concept of Brand Equity   The concept of brand equity is not without its critics (see Feldwick [1996] for some insightful commentary). For example, the principle of "double jeopardy" (DJ) is based on the robust observation that large share brands have more buyers who buy more often and who exhibit unusually high behavioral loyalty (Ehrenberg, Goodhardt, and Barwise 1990; Ehrenberg, Barnard, and Scriven 1997). In downplaying the importance of brand equity, Ehrenberg (1997) interprets this pattern to mean ". . . there are large brands and small ones rather than any evidence of strong brands and weak ones" (p. 10).

Countering this argument, Dyson, Farr, and Hollis (1997) point out that the DJ model describes "aspects of buyer behavior in steady markets with readily substitutable brands" but note that the task of marketing is often to change the setting or situation to the benefit of the brand. In other words, the role of marketing may be to create a violation of double jeopardy patterns. Similarly, Baldinger and Rubinson (1997) maintain that loyalty cannot be assumed and that ". . . in order to become a large brand and stay a large brand, consumers must not only buy it, but like buying it." Finally, Fader and Schmittlein (1993) note that the DJ effect is based in part on an extremely brand-loyal segment for high share brands and their increased availability at retail locations (smaller stores that carry fewer brands are likely to carry the high share brand)—both indicators of brand equity. (See Chaudhuri [1999] for some additional discussion.)

Resolving this debate depends in part on assumptions about market stability and the power of marketing actions to influence consumers. DJ proponents find short-term marketing actions relatively impotent, whereas brand equity proponents believe marketing activities can be disruptive and influence consumer behavior.

Measuring Brand Equity

Keller and Lehmann (2002) provide a broad, integrative perspective on measuring brand equity (see also Srivastava, Shervani, and Fahey 1998; Ambler 2000; Epstein and Westbrook 2001). They describe the "brand value chain" as three steps in the creation of a brand's value. In the first value-creation step, a marketing activity affects the consumer/customer mindset or brand knowledge (via brand awareness, associations, attitudes, attachment, or activity). In the second step, brand knowledge affects market performance (via price premiums and elasticities, cost savings, market share, profitability, and/or expansion success). In the third step, market performance affects shareholder value (via stock price and market capitalization).

Researchers have tried to capture and measure brand equity by measuring each of these outcomes—consumer/customer brand knowledge, product-market performance, and shareholder value, as shown below.

Consumer/Customer Brand Knowledge   Hutchinson, Raman, and Mantrala (1994) develop a general Markov model of brand name recall and explore the implications of three special cases of the model as applied to the soft drinks and beverages categories. Their analysis shows that: (1) market structure plays an important role in determining brand name recall and, as a result, brands in certain situations can therefore be completely ignored; and (2) usage rates, advertising expenditures, market penetration, and various product attributes are found to be significant predictors of recall latency. In a different approach, Duke (1995) shows how indirect memory measures of awareness—the Ebbinghaus Savings Test and word fragment completion—can supplement more traditional measures of free recall.

The Zaltman Metaphor Elicitation Technique (ZMET) uses qualitative methods to tap into consumers' visual and other sensory images of brands (Zaltman and Higie 1993; Zaltman and Coulter 1995). Specifically, ZMET attempts to reveal—via consumers' metaphors for brands—the "mental models" that drive their thinking and behavior. ZMET elicits metaphors by asking consumers to take photographs and/or collect pictures (from magazines, books, and other sources) that indicate what the brand means to them.

Product-Market Performance   Several researchers have applied conjoint analysis to measure aspects of brand equity. For example, Rangaswamy, Burke, and Oliva (1993) use conjoint analysis to explore how brand names interact with physical product features to affect the extendibility of brand names to new product categories. Swait, Erdem, Louviere, and Dubelaar (1993) advocate the design of choice experiments that account for brand name, product attributes, brand image, and differences in consumer socio-demographic characteristics and brand usage. They define the *equalization price*—a proxy for brand equity—as the price that equates the utility of a brand with the utility that can be attributed to a brand in the category where no brand differentiation occurs. They illustrate their approach with an application to the deodorant, athletic shoe, and jeans market.

Using similar techniques, Bello and Holbrook (1995) find comparatively little evidence of price premiums across a number of categories (see also Holbrook 1992), but suggest that this may be due in part to the preponderance of "search" goods as opposed to "experience" goods in their sample. Finally, Mahajan, Rao, and Srivastava (1994) describe a methodology to assess the importance of brand equity in acquisition decisions. They define relative attributes for acquisition such as financial performance, product-market characteristics, and marketing strategy-related variables, and ask key executives to provide ratings of real and hypothetical firms based on that information. They illustrate their approach in the all-suites segment of the hotel industry.

Several researchers employ "residual approaches" to estimate brand equity. In these approaches (e.g., Srinivasan 1979; Bong, Marshall, and Keller 1999), brand equity is what remains of consumer preferences and choices after subtracting objective characteristics of the physical product (some researchers, e.g., Barwise, Higson, Likierman, and Marsh [1989], challenge the separability assumption implicit in these approaches). Kamakura and Russell (1993) employ a single-source, scanner-panel-based measure of brand equity that models consumer choices as a function of two factors: brand value (perceived quality, or the value assigned by consumers to the brand after discounting for current price and recent advertising exposures) and brand intangible value (the component of brand value not directly attributed to the physical product and thus related to brand name associations and "perceptual distortions"). In an application to the laundry detergent market, they show that brand equity is closely related to brand entry order and cumulative advertising expenditures.

Park and Srinivasan (1994) also propose a residual methodology that estimates brand equity by dividing it into two components: (1) the attribute-based component of brand equity, defined as the difference between subjectively perceived attribute values and objectively measured attribute values (e.g., collected from independent testing services such as *Consumer Reports* or acknowledged experts in the field), and (2) the non-attribute-based component of brand equity, defined as the difference between subjectively perceived attribute values and overall preference. They propose a survey procedure to estimate these measures and illustrate their approach in the toothpaste and mouthwash categories.

Dillon, Madden, Kirmani, and Mukherjee (2001) present a model for decomposing brand attribute ratings into two components: brand-specific associations (features, attributes, or benefits that consumers link to a brand) and general brand impressions (overall impressions based on a more holistic view of a brand). They demonstrate their model in three product categories: cars, toothpaste, and paper towels. Finally, using established notions of health found in the epidemiology literature, Bhattacharya and Lodish (2000) define "brand health" in terms of "current well-being" and "resistance." They provide an empirical application of these constructs using store scanner data, demonstrating that their proposed resistance indicator is able to predict the share loss suffered by the existing brands in a category in the event of a new product introduction.

Shareholder Value   Several researchers have studied how the stock market accounts for and reacts to the brand equity of companies and products. Simon and Sullivan (1993) develop a technique for estimating a firm's brand equity derived from financial market estimates of brand-related profits. Based on the assumption that the market value of the firm's securities provides an unbiased estimate of the future cash flows that are attributable to the firm's assets, their estimation technique attempts to extract the value of brand equity from the value of the firm's other assets. They illustrate their approach in part by tracing the brand equity of Coca-Cola and Pepsi over three major events in the soft drink industry from 1982–1986.

Aaker and Jacobson (1994) examine the association between yearly stock return and yearly brand equity changes (as measured by Equi-Trend's perceived quality rating as a proxy for brand equity) for 34 companies during the years 1989–1992, and compare the accompanying changes in current-term return on investment (ROI). They find that, as expected, stock market return is positively related to changes in ROI—but also that stock return is positively related to brand equity. They conclude that investors learn about changes in brand equity (although presumably indirectly through learning about a company's plans and programs) and factor that information into their investment decisions.

Using data for firms in the computer industry in the 1990s, Aaker and Jacobson (2001) find that changes in brand attitude are associated contemporaneously with stock return and lead accounting financial performance. They also find five factors (new products, product problems, competitor actions, changes in top management, and legal actions) that are associated with significant changes in brand attitudes. Similarly, using *Financial World* estimates of brand equity, Barth, Clement, Foster, and

Kasznik (1998) find that brand equity is positively related to stock return and that this effect is incremental to other accounting variables such as the firm's net income.

Adopting an event study methodology, Lane and Jacobson (1995) show that stock market participants' responses to brand extension announcements—consistent with the trade-offs inherent in brand leveraging—depend interactively and non-monotonically on brand attitude and familiarity. Specifically, with their sample, the stock market appears to respond most favorably to extensions of high esteem, high familiarity brands and to low esteem, low familiarity brands (in the latter case, presumably because there was little to risk and much to gain with extensions). The stock market reaction appears to be less favorable (and sometimes even negative) for extensions of brands where consumer familiarity is disproportionately high compared to consumer regard and to extensions of brands where consumer regard is disproportionately high compared to familiarity.

In sum, there are a number of ways to conceptualize and measure brand equity, but all approaches tend to focus on one of three key outcomes that result from brand marketing investments: consumer brand knowledge, product-market performance, or shareholder value. All three outcomes provide insight and can also be related to each other: consumer brand knowledge impacts product-market performance, which, in turn, affects shareholder value. The next section explores some of the components of the brand itself and how they can contribute to brand equity.

Brand Elements

Brand elements are the "trademarkable" devices that identify and differentiate the brand (e.g., brand names, logos, symbols, characters, slogans, jingles, and packages). There are a number of broad criteria for choosing and designing brand elements to build brand equity (Keller 1998). These include memorability, meaningfulness, aesthetic appeal, transferability within and across product categories as well as across geographical and cultural boundaries and market segments, adaptability and flexibility over time, and legal and competitive protectability and defensibility.

Although there is a robust industry to help firms design and implement these elements (see Kohli and LaBahn [1997] for a descriptive account of the brand name selection process), comparatively little academic attention, even in recent years, has been devoted to this topic. Nevertheless, several research studies and programs addressing the design and protection of brand elements have emerged, as follows.

Brand Names

Sensory or Phonetic Considerations   Research on choice criteria for brand names extends back for years (see Robertson [1989] for an overview). A number of studies have considered sensory or phonetic aspects of brand names. For example, in a study of computer-generated brand names containing random combinations of syllables, Peterson and Ross (1972) find that consumers are able to extract at least some product meaning out of these names when instructed to do so. For example, "whumies" and "quax" reminded consumers of a breakfast cereal and "dehax" reminded consumers of a laundry detergent.

Further, some researchers find that even the sounds of individual letters can contain meaning that may be useful in developing a brand name (see Klink [2000] and Yorkston and Menon [2001] for a review of the conceptual mechanisms involved and some managerial applications).

For example, words that begin with "plosives" (e.g., the letters *b*, hard *c*, *d*, *g*, *k*, *p*, and *t*)—which escape from the mouth more quickly and are harsher and more direct than "sibilants" (e.g., the letters *s* and soft *c*)—are thought to make brand names more specific, less abstract, and more easily recognized and recalled (Vanden Bergh, Collins, Schultz, and Adler 1984). In fact, a survey of the top 200 brands in the *Marketing and Media Decision*'s lists for 1971–1985 finds a preponderance of brand names using plosives (Vanden Bergh, Adler, and Oliver 1987). On the other hand, the softer sibilants tend to conjure up romantic, serene images and are often used in the names of products such as perfumes (e.g., Cie, Chanel, and Cerissa) (Doeden 1981). Similarly, Heath, Chatterjee, and Russo (1990) find a relationship between certain characteristics of brand name letters and product features; specifically, as consonant hardness and vowel pitch increase in hypothetical brand names for toilet paper and household cleansers, consumer perception of the product's harshness also increases.

Cultural Aspects   Relatedly, research has examined some cultural and linguistic aspects of brand names. Leclerc, Schmitt, and Dubé (1994) show that certain hypothetical products with brand names that are acceptable in both English and French (e.g., Vaner, Randal, and Massin) are perceived as more "hedonic" (i.e., providing pleasure) and are better liked when pronounced in French than in English, although these effects did not completely generalize in a follow-up replication study (Thakor and Pacheco 1997). Schmitt, Pan, and Tavassoli (1994) show that Chinese speakers are more likely to recall stimuli presented as brand names in visual rather than spoken recall, whereas English speakers are more likely to recall the names in spoken rather than visual recall. They interpret these findings in terms of the fact that mental representations of verbal information in Chinese are coded primarily in a visual manner, whereas verbal information in English is coded primarily in a phonological manner.

Extending that research, Pan and Schmitt (1996) find that matching peripheral feature sounds of a brand name (i.e., "script" aspects such as font or "sound" aspects such as pronunciation) with brand associations or meaning results in more positive brand attitudes than a mismatch. Specifically, Chinese native speakers' attitudes are primarily affected by script matching, and English native speakers' attitudes are primarily affected by sound matching. Similar to the earlier research, Pan and Schmitt interpret these results in terms of structural differences between logographic systems (e.g., Chinese, where characters stand for concepts and not sounds) and alphabetic systems (e.g., English, where letters cue pronunciation) and the respective visual and phonological representations in memory that result.

Finally, Zhang and Schmitt (2001) present a conceptual framework for managing brand name creation in an international, multilingual market, for example, China. Their empirical results indicate that the choice of a translation should be guided by considerations of contextual factors: (1) which brand name (the English or Chinese name) will be emphasized and (2) which translation approach (phonetic, which preserves the sound of the original name, versus phonosemantic, which preserves the sound of the original name and creates product category and brand associations) for similar products is considered the standard in the marketplace.

Semantic Meaning Applying basic associative memory theory, Keller, Heckler, and Houston (1998) show that a brand name that explicitly conveys a product benefit (e.g., PicturePerfect televisions) leads to higher recall of an advertised benefit claim consistent in meaning with the brand name (e.g., picture quality), compared to a non-suggestive brand name (e.g., Emporium televisions). On the other hand, a suggestive brand name leads to lower recall of a subsequently advertised benefit claim unrelated in product meaning (e.g., superior sound), compared to a non-suggestive brand name.

Sen (1999) explores how a brand name's semantic suggestiveness interacts with the decision task involved in an initial encounter with a brand to influence the brand information encoded and recalled during a subsequent encounter with a proposed extension. He finds that when information about an efficient set of new brands is learned through a choice task (i.e., no brand dominated its competitors), brand names that suggest general superiority appear to benefit subsequent brand extensions more than names that are suggestive of category-specific, attribute-based superiority. After a judgment task, however, the category-specific names appear to benefit brand extensions more than the general superiority names.

Finally, in an exploratory study of alpha-numeric brand names, that is, containing one or more numbers in either digit form (e.g., 5) or in written form (e.g., five), Pavia and Costa (1993) find that alpha-numeric brand names are more favorably evaluated when designating technology-related products. This effect is moderated by a number of factors, including the visual or aural aspects of the name, the actual numbers that are used in the name, and the words or letters, along with the number(s), that comprise the brand name.

Logos

Little academic research has explored the consumer behavior effects of logo design or other visual aspects of branding (see Schmitt and Simonson [1997] for some background discussion). Henderson and Cote (1998) conduct a comprehensive empirical analysis of 195 logos that are calibrated on 13 different design characteristics in terms of their ability to achieve different communication objectives. Their results suggest the following: more complex and elaborate logos are better at maintaining viewer interest and liking; logos with uniformity along a single dimension are more likely to be falsely recognized; and familiar logos are better liked than unfamiliar logos (Janiszewski and Meyvis 2001).

Janiszewski and Meyvis (2001) suggest that a dual-process model is most applicable in describing consumer responses to repeated exposure to static brand names, logos, and packages. The dual-process model assumes a passive processing system by consumers and posits that their response to a stimulus is a function of sensitization and habituation. They provide experimental evidence to that effect.

Legal Considerations

Several academics consider legal issues involved with branding. Cohen (1986, 1991) argues that trademark strategy involves proper trademark planning, implementation, and control. Zaichkowsky (1995) provides a comprehensive treatment of brand confusion (see also Foxman, Berger, and Cote 1992). Simonson (1994) provides an in-depth discussion of these issues and methods to assess the likelihood of confusion and "genericness" of a trademark. He stresses that consumers may vary in their level or degree of confusion and that, as a result, it is difficult to identify a precise threshold level above which confusion "occurs." He also notes that survey research methods to assess confusion must accurately reflect the consumers' states of mind when engaged in marketplace activities.

Simonson provides behavioral perspectives to consider a number of issues related to trademark dilution (e.g., Simonson 1995). Harvey, Rothe, and Lucas (1998) consider the legal and strategic implications of the look-a-like "trade dress" practice of major food chains that adopt the visual cues (e.g., shape, size, color, and the like) of national brands in branding their private labels (see also Kapferer 1995; Loken, Ross, and Hinkle 1986). Oakenfull and Gelb (1996) describe how to avoid "genericide" (when consumers employ the brand name as the product category label) through research and advertising. Finally, Sullivan (2001) considers the optimal number of registered trademarks to protect a brand.

In short, the components or elements that make up the brand can individually and collectively impact brand equity and must be designed and implemented carefully with those goals in mind. Next, we turn to considerations concerning brand intangibles and how brands can have more abstract associations that provide valuable means of differentiation.

Brand Intangibles

Brand intangibles—the aspects of brand image that do not involve physical, tangible, or concrete attributes or benefits—are an important and relatively unique aspect of branding research (for a review of some seminal work in this area, see Levy [1999]). Brand intangibles are often a means by which marketers differentiate their brands (Park, Jaworski, and MacInnis 1986) and transcend, or go beyond, physical product characteristics (Kotler 2000), and can be examined at both the product-brand and corporate-brand levels.

Product-Brand Level

Brand Personality   Brand personality is defined as the human characteristics or traits that can be attributed to a brand. Aaker (1997) examines 114 possible personality traits and 37 well-known brands in various product categories to create a brand personality scale composed of five factors: sincerity (e.g., down-to-earth, honest, wholesome, and cheerful), excitement (e.g., daring, spirited, imaginative, and up-to-date), competence (e.g., reliable, intelligent, and successful), sophistication (e.g., upper class and charming), and ruggedness (e.g., outdoorsy and tough). In a cross-cultural study exploring the generalizability of this scale outside the U.S., Aaker, Benet-Martínez, and Berrocal (2001) find that three of the five factors applied in Japan and Spain, but that a "peacefulness" dimension replaces "ruggedness" both in Japan and Spain and a "passion" dimension emerges in Spain instead of "competence."

Aaker (1999) suggests that consumer preference for, and use of, brands will vary across usage situations, based on brand personality associations. She finds that brands that are highly self-congruent (that is, brand personality matches those of subjects) are preferred by consumers who are low self-monitoring (that is, the extent to which their behavior is guided by situational cues to social appropriateness is low), whereas brands that are highly situation-congruent (that is, brand personality matches the situation) are preferred by consumers who are high self-monitoring (that is, the extent to which their behavior is guided by situational cues is high).

Relatedly, Graeff (1996) finds that, as consumers' self-monitoring increases, their evaluations of publicly consumed, but not privately consumed, brands are more affected by brand image self-congruence. Moreover, consumers' evaluations of publicly consumed brands are also more affected by the congruence between brand image and ideal self-image than actual self-image. In the case of privately consumed brands, however, these effects are equal. Graeff (1997) extends these findings to show that ideal self-image can vary by situation and that congruence between ideal self-image and brand image should be measured situation-specific (e.g., dinner with a boss versus with a friend).

Brand Experience Arguing that marketers and brand managers have largely ignored sensory, affective, and creative experiences, Schmitt (1997) develops the SOOP ("superficial—out of profundity") model of the branding of customer experiences. He distinguishes between three types of experiential brands—"sense," "feel," and "think"—based on their primary appeal and the type of experience they target. Schmitt argues that common to all types of brands is the idea of providing value to consumers by enhancing relations between the brand and the consumer through "experience providers" that include communications, visual and verbal identity, product presence, co-branding, spatial environment, web sites and electronic media, and people. He also defines five types of sensory experiences (or "strategic experiential modules"): "sense" experiences involving sensory perception, "feel" experiences involving affect and emotions, "think" experiences which are creative and cognitive, "act" experiences involving the physical and possibly incorporating individual actions and lifestyles, and "relate" experiences resulting from connecting with a reference group or culture. (See also Schmitt 1999a, b.)

Brand Relationships Fournier (1998) extends the metaphor of interpersonal relationships into the brand domain to conceptualize the relationships that consumers form with brands (see also Fournier and Yao 1997; Fournier, Dobscha, and Mick 1998). Fournier views brand relationship quality as multifaceted; she delineates six dimensions beyond loyalty/commitment along which consumer-brand relationships vary: self-concept connection, commitment or nostalgic attachment, behavioral interdependence, love/passion, intimacy, and brand partner quality. Based on lengthy, in-depth consumer interviews, Fournier defines 15 possible consumer-brand relationship forms: arranged marriages, casual friends/buddies, marriages of convenience, committed partnerships, best friendships, compartmentalized friendships, kinships, rebounds/avoidance-driven relationships, childhood friendships, courtships, dependencies, flings, enmities, secret affairs, and enslavements. Additionally, Fournier (2000) develops the Brand Relationship Quality scale to empirically capture these theoretical notions.

Aaker, Benet-Martínez, and Berrocal (2001) conduct a two-month longitudinal investigation of the development and evolution of relationships between consumers and brands, and find that two factors—experience of a transgression and personality of the brand—have a significant influence on developmental form and dynamics. Specifically, brands associated with "sincerity" traits relative to those that with "excitement" traits demonstrate increasing levels of relationship strength over time, but those results hold only when the relationship develops without the experience of a transgression. In cases where a transgression occurs, relationship strength dramatically suffers for sincere brands; however, some aspects of relationship strength eventually rebound for exciting brands.

Brand Communities Muniz and O'Guinn (2001) define a "brand community" as a specialized, non-geographically bound community, based on a structured set of social relationships among users of a brand. They note that, like other communities, a brand community is marked by a shared consciousness, rituals and traditions, and a sense of moral responsibility. They demonstrate these characteristics in both face-to-face and computer-mediated environments for the Apple Macintosh, Ford Bronco, and Saab brands.

Relatedly, Schouten and McAlexander (1995) define a "subculture of consumption" as a distinctive subgroup of society that self-selects on the basis of a shared commitment to a particular product class, brand, or consumption activity. They note that characteristics of a subculture of consumption include an identifiable, hierarchical social structure, a unique ethos or set of shared beliefs and values, and unique jargons, rituals, and modes of symbolic expression. To illustrate, they present results of a three-year ethnographic field study with Harley-Davidson motorcycle owners. They later expand their investigation to include the Jeep brand and explore various relationships that consumers could have with the product/possession, brand, firm, and/or other customers as a measure of loyalty (McAlexander, Schouten, and Koenig 2002).

Corporate-Brand Level

Corporate Image   Much research has considered corporate image in terms of its conceptualization, antecedents, and consequences (e.g., see reviews by Barich and Kotler 1991; Biehal and Sheinin 1998; Dowling 1994; Schumann, Hathcote, and West 1991). A corporate image can be thought of as consumers' associations with the company or corporation making the product or providing the service as a whole. Corporate image is a particularly relevant concern when the corporate or company brand plays a prominent role in the branding strategy. A corporate brand may evoke associations wholly different from an individual brand, which is only identified with a certain product or limited set of products (Brown 1998).

For example, a corporate brand name may be more likely to evoke associations of common products and their shared attributes or benefits, people and relationships, and programs and values. Brown and Dacin (1997) distinguish between corporate associations related to corporate ability (i.e., expertise in producing and delivering product and/or service offering) and corporate social responsibility (i.e., character of the company with regard to important societal issues). Regarding the latter, much research explores the implications of cause-related marketing (e.g., Drumwright 1996; Sen and Bhattacharya 2001; Varadarajan and Menon 1988) and "green" marketing strategies (e.g., *Journal of Advertising* 1995; Menon and Menon 1997).

Keller and Aaker (1992, 1998) define corporate credibility as the extent to which consumers believe that a company is willing and able to deliver products and services that satisfy customer needs and wants. Based on past consumer behavior research (e.g., Sternthal and Craig 1984), they identify three possible dimensions to corporate credibility: *corporate expertise*—the extent to which a company is seen as being able to competently make and sell their products or conduct their services; *corporate trustworthiness*—the extent to which the company is seen as motivated to be honest, dependable, and sensitive to consumer needs; and *corporate likability*—the extent to which the company is seen as likable, prestigious, interesting, etc.

Experimentally, Keller and Aaker (1992) show that successfully introduced brand extensions can enhance perceptions of corporate credibility and can improve evaluations of even more dissimilar brand extensions. Keller and Aaker (1998) show that different types of corporate marketing activity, by impacting different dimensions of corporate credibility as well as perceptions of extension fit and attribute beliefs, differentially affect consumer evaluations of a corporate brand extension. Specifically, corporate marketing activity related to product innovation produces more favorable evaluations for a corporate brand extension than corporate marketing activity related to either the environment or, especially, the community. Their findings also reveal that corporate marketing activity influences evaluations even in the presence of advertising for the extension (see also Brown and Dacin 1997).

Thus far, the focus has been on the fundamental concepts that underlie our understanding of brand equity and how it is measured, as well as the effects of the components that make up the brand and the intangible associations that transcend the concrete or tangible aspects of the brand. Next, we consider how firms can leverage the equity that they have created to enter new product categories via brand extensions.

Brand Extensions

The branding research area that has received the most attention in recent years is how firms should leverage brand equity, especially in terms of brand extensions.

Basic Processes

Modeling Consumer Evaluations of Brand Extensions   Much research has adopted a categorization perspective in modeling consumer evaluations of brand extensions (e.g., Boush and Loken 1991; Hartman, Price, and Duncan 1990; Loken and John 1993). According to this perspective, if a brand introduces an extension that is seen as closely related or similar in "fit" to the brand category, then consumers can easily transfer their existing attitude about the parent brand to the extension. On the other hand, if consumers are not certain about extension similarity, they may evaluate the extension in a more detailed, "piecemeal," or constructive fashion, and specific associations they infer about the extension would be the primary determinants of their evaluation.

Fit is thus identified as a key moderator of how consumers evaluate consumer evaluations of brand extensions (Boush, Shipp, Loken, Gencturk, Crockett, Kennedy, Minshall, Misurell, Rochford, and Strobel 1987). Consistent with this notion, Aaker and Keller (1990) find that a perception of fit between the original parent brand and extension product categories as well as a perception of high quality for the parent brand leads to more favorable extension evaluations. A number of subsequent studies explore the generalizability of these findings to markets outside the U.S. Based on a comprehensive analysis of 131 brand extensions from seven such replication studies around the world, Bottomley and Holden (2001) conclude that this basic model clearly generalizes, although cross-cultural differences influence the relative importance attached to the model components. In examining why some brands are able to extend into "perceptually distinct" domains, however, Klink and Smith (2001) show that effects of fit can disappear when attribute information is added to extension stimuli and are applicable only for later product adopters, and that perceived fit increases with greater exposure to an extension.

On the other hand, applying Mandler's congruity theory, Meyers-Levy, Louie, and Curren (1994) show that suggested products associated with moderately incongruent brand names can be preferred over ones that are associated with either congruent or extremely incongruent brand names (see also Zinkhan and Martin 1987). They interpret this finding in terms of the ability of moderately incongruent brand extensions to elicit more processing from consumers that could be satisfactorily resolved (assuming consumers could identify a meaningful relationship between the brand name and the product).

Bases of Extension Fit Prior research examines a number of different factors concerning fit perceptions. In general, this research reinforces the importance of taking a broad and contextual view of fit. Adopting a demand-side and supply-side perspective, Aaker and Keller (1990) show that perceived fit between a parent brand and extension product could be related to the economic notions of perceived substitutability and complementarity in product use (from a demand-side perspective), as well as the perceived ability of the firm to have the skills and assets necessary to make the extension product (from a supply-side perspective).

Subsequent research shows that virtually any association for a parent brand held in memory by consumers may serve as a potential basis of fit. Park, Milberg, and Lawson (1991) distinguish between fit based on "product-feature-similarity" and "brand-concept-consistency" (that is, how well the brand concept accommodates the extension product). They also distinguish between function-oriented brands, whose dominant associations relate to product performance (e.g., Timex watches), and prestige-oriented brands, whose dominant associations relate to consumers' expression of self-concept or image (e.g., Rolex watches). Experimentally, Park, Milberg, and Lawson show that the Rolex brand can more easily extend into categories such as grandfather clocks, bracelets, and rings than the Timex brand; but Timex can more easily extend into categories such as stopwatches, batteries, and calculators than Rolex.

They interpret these results to suggest that, for Rolex, high brand-concept consistency overcomes a lack of product-feature similarity; and for Timex, product-feature similarity favors a function-oriented brand.

Broniarczyk and Alba (1994) show that even a brand that is not as favorably evaluated as a competing brand in its category may, depending on the particular parent brand associations involved, be more success-fully extended into certain categories. For example, in their study, Close-Up toothpaste is not as well liked as Crest toothpaste; however, a proposed Close-Up breath mint extension is evaluated more favorably than one from Crest. Alternatively, a proposed Crest toothbrush exten-sion is evaluated more favorably than one from Close-Up.

Broniarczyk and Alba (1994) also show that a perceived lack of fit between the parent brand's product category and the proposed extension category can be overcome if key parent brand associations are deemed valuable in the extension category. For example, Froot Loops cereal, which has strong brand associations to "sweet," "flavor," and "kids," is bet-ter able to extend to dissimilar product categories such as lollipops and popsicles than to even similar product categories such as waffles and hot cereal because of the relevance of their brand associations in the dissim-ilar extension category. The reverse is true for Cheerios cereal, however, which has a "healthy grain" association that is only relevant in similar extension product categories.

Thus, extension fit is more than just the number of common and dis-tinctive brand associations between the parent brand and the extension product category (e.g., see Bijmolt, Wedel, Pieters, and DeSarbo 1998). Along these lines, Bridges, Keller, and Sood (2000) refer to "category coherence" of extensions. Coherent categories are those categories whose members "hang together" and "make sense." According to this view, to understand the rationale for a grouping of products in a brand line, a consumer needs "explanatory links" that tie the products together and summarize their relationship. For example, the physically dissimilar toy, bath care, and car seat products in the Fisher-Price product line can be united by the link, "products for children."

Similarly, Schmitt and Dubé (1992) propose that brand extensions should be viewed as conceptual combinations. A conceptual combination (e.g., "apartment dog") consists of a modifying concept or "modifier" (e.g., apartment) and a modified concept or "header" (e.g., dog). Thus, according to this view, a proposed brand extension such as McDonald's Theme Park would be interpreted as the original brand or company name (McDonald's) acting on the "head concept" of the extension category (theme parks) as a "modifier." Bristol (1996) adopts a similar view and suggests that consumers often seem to construct on-line "conjunctive inferences" about extensions without exclusively using knowledge about the retrieved brand, product class, product-type category or subcategory, or exemplar or noteworthy brand.

Finally, research has explored other more specific aspects of fit. Boush (1997) provides experimental data as to the context sensitivity of fit judgments. Similarity judgments between pairs of product categories are found to be asymmetrical, and brand name associations can reverse the direction of asymmetry. For example, more subjects agree with the statement "*Time* magazine is like Time books" than the statement "Time books are like *Time* magazine," but without the brand names, the preferences are reversed. Smith and Andrews (1995) survey industrial goods marketers and find that the relationship between fit and new product evaluations is not direct but is mediated by customers' sense of certainty that a firm could provide a proposed new product. Finally, Martin and Stewart (2001) explore the multidimensional nature of product similarity ratings and the moderating effects of goal congruency. They show that extensions may not be successful even when they appear similar to the core product if consumers do not link the extension with a goal also associated with the core brand. In that light, they argue that Nike's failed extension into dress leather shoes may reflect the fact that the extension didn't tap into goals related to athletic performance, as is the case with the core brand.

Extension Feedback Effects   Much research has considered the reciprocal effects on the parent brand from an extension. Keller and Aaker (1992) and Romeo (1991) find that unsuccessful extensions in dissimilar product categories do not affect evaluations of the parent brand. The Keller and Aaker study also shows that unsuccessful extensions do not necessarily prevent a company from "retrenching" and later introducing a more similar extension. Sullivan (1990) finds that the "sudden acceleration" problems associated with the Audi 5000 automobile had greater spillover to the Audi 4000 model than to the Audi Quattro model, which she interprets as a result of the fact that the latter was branded and marketed differently.

Loken and John (1993) find that dilution effects (where parent brand evaluations and associations become less favorable) are evident, but only under certain conditions (e.g., when extensions are perceived to be moderately typical of the parent brand and when extension typicality is not made salient to consumers) and for certain types of beliefs (e.g., gentleness beliefs rather than quality beliefs). In their study, however, dilution effects are largely unrelated to the similarity of the brand extension. John, Loken, and Joiner (1998) find that dilution effects are less likely to be present with "flagship" products, and can occur with line extensions but are not always evident for more dissimilar category extensions.

Gürhan-Canli and Maheswaran (1998) extend the results of these studies by considering the moderating effect of consumer motivation and extension typicality and congruency. They define typicality as the degree to which category members (i.e., different products manufactured by Sony or Sanyo) are representative of the family brand image. They define congruency as the extent to which product information provided is consistent or inconsistent with prior expectations (e.g., positive information conveyed about Sony). In high motivation conditions, they find that incongruent extensions are scrutinized in detail and lead to the modification of family brand evaluations, regardless of the typicality of the extensions. In low motivation conditions, however, brand evaluations are more extreme in the context of high (versus low) typicality. As the less typical extension is considered an exception, its impact on family brand evaluations is reduced. In a similar vein, Ahluwalia and Gürhan-Cali (2000) adopt an accessibility-diagnosticity perspective to explain the effects of brand extensions on the family brand name and observe comparable experimental results. Finally, Milberg, Park, and McCarthy (1997) find that negative feedback effects are present when: (1) extensions are perceived as belonging to a product category dissimilar from those associated with the family brand and (2) extension attribute information is inconsistent with image beliefs associated with the family brand.

In terms of individual differences, Lane and Jacobson (1997) find some evidence of a negative reciprocal impact from brand extensions, especially for high need-for-cognition subjects, but do not explore extension similarity differences. Kirmani, Sood, and Bridges (1999) find dilution effects with owners of prestige image automobiles when low-priced extensions are introduced but not with owners of non-prestige automobiles or with non-owners of either type of automobile. Using national household scanner data, Swaminathan, Fox, and Reddy (2001) find positive reciprocal effects of extension trial on parent brand choice, particularly among non-loyal users and prior non-users of the parent brand, and consequently on market share. Category similarity, however, appears to moderate the existence and magnitude of these effects. Evidence is also found for potential negative effects of unsuccessful extensions among prior users of the parent brand but not prior non-users. Additionally, experience with the parent brand is found to have significant impact on extension trial, but not on extension repeat.

Morrin (1999) examines the impact of brand extensions on the strength of parent brand associations in memory. Two computer-based studies reveal that exposing consumers to brand extension information strengthens rather than weakens parent brand associations in memory, particularly for parent brands that are dominant in their original product category. Higher fit also results in greater facilitation of parent brand recall but only for non-dominant parent brands. Moreover, improvements in parent brand memory due to the advertised introduction of an extension is not as great as when the same level of advertising directly promotes the parent brand.

In reviewing this literature, Keller and Sood (2001a) put forth a conceptual model that posits that changes in consumer evaluations of a parent brand as a result of the introduction of a brand extension is a function of three factors: strength and clarity of extension evidence, diagnosticity or relevance of extension evidence, and evaluative consistency of extension evidence with parent brand associations. One implication of their conceptual model is that existing parent brand knowledge structures, in general, will be fairly resistant to change: In order for parent brand associations to change, consumers must be confronted with compelling evidence that is seen as relevant to existing parent brand associations, and they must be convinced that the evidence is inconsistent enough to warrant a change (John, Loken, and Joiner 1998).

Thus, an unsuccessful brand extension can potentially damage the parent brand only when there is a high degree of similarity or "fit" involved, for example, in the case of a failed line extension in the same category. When the brand extension is farther removed, consumers can "compartmentalize" the brand's products and disregard its performance in what is seen as an unrelated product category. Keller and Sood (2001a) provide experimental evidence consistent with all of these conjectures.

Types of Brand Extensions

Line Extensions   Prior research (Farquhar 1989; Keller 1998) distinguishes between line extensions (i.e., when the parent brand is used to brand a new product that targets a new market segment within a product category currently served by the parent brand) and category extensions (i.e., when the parent brand is used to enter a different product category from that currently served by the parent brand). Several studies examine the market performance of real brands to determine the success characteristics of line extensions (see Quelch and Kenny [1994] for some useful managerial insights and guidelines and Hardie, Lodish, Kilmer, Beatty, Farris, Biel, Wicke, Balson, and Aaker [1994] for commentary).

Using data on 75 line extensions of 34 cigarette brands over a 20-year period, Reddy, Holak, and Bhat (1994) find that:

- Line extensions of strong brands are more successful than line extensions of weak brands.

- Line extensions of symbolic brands enjoy greater market success than those of less symbolic brands.

- Line extensions that receive strong advertising and promotional support are more successful than line extensions that receive meager support.

- Line extensions entering earlier into a product subcategory are more successful than line extensions entering later, but only if they are line extensions from strong brands.

- Firm size and marketing competencies also play a part in a line extension's success.

- Earlier line extensions help in the market expansion of the parent brand.

- Incremental sales generated by line extensions can more than compensate for the loss in sales due to cannibalization.

Based on data collected from 166 product managers in packaged goods firms, Andrews and Low (1998) find that meaningful product line extensions are launched in companies that have longer planning and reward horizons, encourage risk taking, rotate brand assignments regularly, have a product-focused management structure, require comparatively more evidence to justify new SKUs, and utilize smaller new product development teams.

In an empirical study of the determinants of product line decisions in the personal computer industry from 1981–1992, Putsis and Bayus (2001) find that firms in the personal computer industry expand their product lines when there are low industry barriers (e.g., few market-wide introductions, low industry concentration) or perceived market opportunities (e.g., due to high market share, recent market entry). High market share firms are found to aggressively expand their product lines, as are firms with relatively high prices or short existing product lines. They also find important substantive differences between the factors affecting the direction of a product line change (i.e., expansion or contraction of its current line) and the magnitude of any line change (i.e., how many products are introduced or withdrawn).

In the context of fast-moving packaged goods, Cohen, Eliashberg, and Ho (1997) develop a decision support system to evaluate the financial prospects of potential new line extensions. The model incorporates historical knowledge about the productivity of the firm's new product development process, as well as research and development resource factors that affect productivity, to provide shipment forecasts at various stages, allow for a product line perspective, and facilitate organizational learning.

Vertical Extensions   For market or competitive considerations, firms often introduce lower-priced versions of their established brand name products. Additionally, some marketers attempt to migrate their brand up-market through brand extensions. Many strategic recommendations have been offered regarding such "vertical extensions" (e.g., Aaker 1997). For example, Farquhar, Han, Herr, and Ijiri (1992) describe how to use "sub-branding" strategies as a means to distinguish lower-priced entries and "super-branding" strategies to signal a noticeable, although presumably not dramatic, quality improvement (e.g., Ultra Dry Pampers). Comparatively little empirical academic research, however, has been conducted on this topic.

In an empirical study of the U.S. mountain bicycle industry, Randall, Ulrich, and Reibstein (1998) find that brand price premium is significantly positively correlated with the quality of the lowest quality model in the product line for the lower quality segments of the market; and that for the upper quality segments of the market, brand price premium is also significantly positively correlated with the quality of the highest quality model in the product line. They conclude that managers wishing only to maximize the equity of their brands will offer only high quality products and avoid offering low quality products, although overall profit maximization could dictate a different strategy (involving a tradeoff between preserving high brand equity—and therefore high margins—and pursuing the volume typically located in the lower end of the market).

Kirmani, Sood, and Bridges (1999) examine the "ownership effect"— in which owners have more favorable responses than non-owners to brand extensions—in the context of brand line stretches. They find that the ownership effect occurs for upward and downward stretches of non-prestige brands (e.g., Acura) and for upward stretches of prestige brands (e.g., Calvin Klein and BMW). For downward stretches of prestige brands, however, the ownership effect does not occur because of owners' desire to maintain brand exclusivity. In this situation, a sub-branding strategy protects owners' parent brand attitudes from dilution.

Multiple Brand Extensions   Keller and Aaker (1992) show that when consumers do not already have strongly held attitudes, the successful introduction of a brand extension improves evaluations of a parent brand that was originally perceived only to be of average quality. By changing the image and meaning of the brand, the successfully introduced extension also could make *subsequent* brand extensions that otherwise may not have seemed appropriate to consumers to make more sense and to be seen as a better fit. Experimentally, they show that by taking "little steps," i.e., by introducing a series of closely related but increasingly distant extensions, it is possible for a brand to enter product categories that would be much more difficult, or perhaps even impossible, to enter directly. For example, a maker of potato chips could introduce a line of ice cream if they had already successfully extended into cheese crackers and then into cookies. Similarly, Dawar and Anderson (1994) show that undertaking extension introductions in a particular order allows distant extensions to be perceived as coherent and that following a consistent direction in extension strategy allows for greater coherence and purchase likelihood for a target extension (see also Jap 1993).

Boush and Loken (1991) find that far extensions from a "broad" brand are evaluated more favorably than from a "narrow" brand. Relatedly, Dacin and Smith (1994) show that if the perceived quality levels of different members of a brand portfolio are more uniform, then consumers tend to make higher, more confident evaluations of a proposed new extension. They also show that a firm that demonstrates little variance in quality across a diverse set of product categories is better able to overcome perceptions of lack of extension fit (i.e., as if consumers think, "whatever they do, they tend to do well").

Dawar (1996) shows that for brands with a single product association, brand knowledge and context interact to influence evaluations of fit for extensions to products that are only weakly associated with the brand. Specifically, retrieval inhibition effects appear to reduce the activation of "less relevant" product associations, lowering perceived fit of extensions close to such products, especially for individuals more knowledgeable about the brand. For brands strongly associated with more than one product, only context—by selectively eliciting retrieval of brand associations—influences the evaluations of the extension fit.

In an empirical study of 95 brands in 11 non-durable consumer goods categories, Sullivan (1992) finds that, in terms of stages of the product category life cycle, early-entering brand extensions do not perform as well, on average, as either early-entering new-name products or late-entering brand extensions. DeGraba and Sullivan (1995) provide an economic analysis to help interpret this observation. They posit that the major source of uncertainty in introducing a new product is the inability to know if it will be a commercial success. They further argue that this uncertainty can be mitigated by spending more time on the development process. Under such assumptions, they show that the large spillover effects triggered by introducing a poorly received brand extension cause introducers of brand extensions to spend more time on the development process than do introducers of new-name products. Finally, Sullivan (1990) finds that when Jaguar launched its first new model in 17 years, the older models of Jaguar experienced an increase in demand as a result of advertising used to promote the new 1988 model.

Moderating Factors

Characteristics of Consumers   Perceptions of fit and extension evaluations may depend on how much consumers know about the product categories involved. Muthukrishnan and Weitz (1990) show that knowledgeable, "expert" consumers are more likely to use technical or manufacturing commonalities to judge fit, considering similarity in terms of technology, design and fabrication, and the materials and components used in the manufacturing process. Less knowledgeable "novice" consumers are more likely to use superficial, perceptual considerations such as common package, shape, color, size, usage, etc. Relatedly, Broniarczyk and Alba (1994) show that perceptions of fit on the basis of brand-specific associations are contingent on consumers having the necessary knowledge about the parent brand. Without such knowledge, consumers again tend to rely on more superficial considerations, such as their level of awareness for the brand or overall regard for the parent brand, in forming extension evaluations. Finally, Zhang and Sood (2002) show that 11- to 12-year-old consumers, relative to adults, evaluate brand extensions by relying less on category similarity between the parent brand and the extension category, and more on the inherent characteristics of the name itself used to brand the extension. Thus, whether the extension is close or far does not matter as much to children as whether or not it rhymes (e.g., a Coca-Cola extension called "Gola" is liked better by children than one called "Higley") (see also Achenreiner and John 2002; Nguyen and John 2001).

In a cross-cultural study, Han and Schmitt (1997) find that for U.S. consumers, perceived fit is more important than company size in extension evaluations, but that for Hong Kong consumers, company size matters for low fit extensions. They suggest that the value of collectivism may explain the relative higher importance of corporate identity as a quality cue for East Asian consumers.

Characteristics of the Parent Brand   Perceptions of fit and extension evaluations may also depend on characteristics of the parent brand. Prior research has shown that one important benefit of building a strong brand is that it can be extended more easily into more diverse categories (e.g., Rangaswamy, Burke, and Oliva 1993). High quality brands are often seen as more credible, expert, and trustworthy (Keller and Aaker 1992). As a result, even though consumers may believe a relatively distant extension does not really fit with the brand, they may be more willing to give a high quality brand the benefit of the doubt. When a brand is seen as average in quality, however, such favorable source attributions may be less forthcoming, and consumers may be more likely to question the ability or motives of the company involved.

As a caveat to the previous conclusion, prior research (e.g., Farquhar and Herr 1992) has shown that if a brand is seen as representing or exemplifying a category overly, it may be difficult for consumers to think of the brand in any other way, making it difficult to extend into a different category. Farquhar, Han, Herr, and Ijiri (1992) define a master brand as an established brand so dominant in customers' minds that it "owns" a particular association, that is, the mention of a product attribute or category, a usage situation, or a customer benefit instantly brings a master brand to mind (e.g., Arm & Hammer baking soda, JELL-O gelatin, Campbell's soup, Morton salt, and Bacardi rum). Since such associations may make it difficult for a master brand to extend to other product categories, they propose branding strategies to extend master brands *indirectly* by leveraging alternative master brand associations that come from different parts of their brand hierarchies, for example, via sub-branding (e.g., Johnnie Walker Red Label, Black Label, and Gold Label scotch whiskey), super-branding (e.g., Extra Strength Tylenol), brand-bundling (e.g., Citibank AAdvantage Visa card), and brand-bridging (e.g., endorsed brands such as Fairfield Inn by Marriott).

The extension limits faced by master brands may be exacerbated by the fact that, in many cases, brands that are market leaders have strong concrete product attribute associations (Farquhar, Han, Herr, and Ijiri 1992). In general, concrete attribute associations may not transfer as broadly to other extension categories than more abstract attribute associations. For example, Aaker and Keller (1990) show that consumers dismiss a hypothetical Heineken popcorn extension as potentially tasting bad or like beer, a hypothetical Vidal Sassoon perfume extension as having an undesirably strong shampoo scent, and a hypothetical Crest chewing gum extension as tasting like toothpaste or, more generally, tasting unappealing. In each case, consumers infer a concrete negative attribute association with a technically feasible extension—even though common sense suggests that a manufacturer would not introduce a product extension with such an attribute.

On the other hand, more abstract associations may be seen as more relevant across a wide set of categories (Rangaswamy, Burke, and Oliva 1993). For example, the Aaker and Keller study also shows that the Vuarnet brand has a remarkable ability to be exported to a disparate set of product categories, e.g., sportswear, watches, wallets, and even skis. In these cases, complementarity may lead to an inference that the extension will have the "stylish" attribute associated with the Vuarnet name, and such an association is valued in the different extension contexts.

Two caveats should be noted, however, concerning the relative extendibility of concrete and abstract associations. First, concrete attributes can be transferred to *some* product categories (Herr, Farquhar, and Fazio 1996). Farquhar et al. (1992) argue that if the parent brand has a concrete attribute association that is highly valued in the extension category because it creates a distinctive taste, ingredient, or component, an extension on that basis can often be successful. Second, abstract associations may not always transfer easily. Bridges, Keller, and Sood (2000) examine the relative transferability of product-related brand information when it was either represented as an abstract brand association (e.g., durable) or as concrete brand associations (e.g., water-resistant quartz movements and shatter-proof crystal for a watch). Surprisingly, the two types of brand images extend equally well into a dissimilar product category, in part because subjects did not seem to believe that the abstract benefit would have the same meaning in the extension category (e.g., durability may be equally relevant in the categories of watches and handbags, although it does not necessarily "transfer" from watches to handbags as the durability means different things).

Finally and relatedly, Joiner and Loken (1998), in a demonstration of the inclusion effect in a brand extension setting, show that consumers often generalize possession of an attribute from a specific category (e.g., Sony televisions) to a more general category (e.g., all Sony products) more readily than they generalize to another specific category (e.g., Sony bicycles). This inclusion effect is attenuated when the specific extension category increases its typicality to the general category (e.g., Sony cameras versus Sony bicycles, that is, there is more "transfer" for cameras than bikes).

Characteristics of the Extension Category   Prior research shows that some seemingly appropriate extensions may be dismissed because of the nature of the extension product involved. If the product is seen as comparatively easy to make—such that brand differences are hard to come by—then consumers may see a high quality brand as incongruous or, alternatively, may feel that the brand extension will attempt to command an unreasonable price premium. For example, Aaker and Keller (1990) show that hypothetical extensions such as Heineken popcorn, Vidal Sassoon perfume, Crest shaving cream, and Häagen-Dazs cottage cheese receive relatively poor marks from experimental subjects in part because *all* brands in the extension category are seen as being about the same in quality, suggesting that the proposed brand extension is unlikely to be superior to existing products. When the extension category is seen as difficult to make, on the other hand, such that brands potentially vary a great deal in quality, there is a greater opportunity for a brand extension to differentiate itself, although consumers may also be less sure as to the quality level of the extension (Kardes and Allen 1990).

Other researchers have looked at the choice context faced by the extension in the new category. For example, Heath, McCarthy, and Milberg

(2001) find that the advantages of a brand extension (e.g., Sony cameras) over a suggestive new brand name (e.g., Optix cameras) are confined to situations of limited information processing and better fit. When consumers have more product attribute information, the nature of the brand name (new versus extension) has little effect. When consumers process information more deeply, new brands can perform as well as or better than brand extensions. The researchers also find differences in their experimental study between consumer attitudes and their choices, suggesting an important caveat to generalizations from lab studies. (See also Hem and Iverson 2001.)

Characteristics of the Extension Marketing Program   Prior research suggests that introductory marketing programs for extensions can be more effective than if the new product is launched with a new name (Kerin, Kalyanaram, and Howard 1996; Smith 1992; Smith and Park 1992). Moreover, a number of studies show that the information provided about brand extensions through its supporting marketing programs, by triggering selective retrieval from memory, may "frame" the consumer decision process and affect extension evaluations (see Boush 1993).

For example, Aaker and Keller (1990) find that cueing or reminding consumers about the quality of a parent brand does not improve evaluations for poorly rated extensions. Because the parent brands are well known and well liked, quality reminders may not offer "new" information to consumers' evaluations of the extensions. However, elaborating briefly on specific extension attributes about which consumers are uncertain or concerned appears to be effective in inhibiting negative inferences and in reducing the salience of consumers' concerns about the firm's credibility in the extension context, thus leading to more favorable evaluations.

Bridges, Keller, and Sood (2000) find that providing information improves perceptions of fit in two cases when consumers perceive low fit between a parent brand and an extension. When the parent brand and the extension share physical attributes but the parent brand image is non-product-related and based on abstract user characteristics, consumers tend to overlook an obvious explanatory link between the parent brand and extension (e.g., a tennis shoe with a high fashion image attempting to extend to work boots may not be evaluated favorably).

Information that raised the salience of the physical relationship relative to distracting non-product-related associations—a "relational" communication strategy—improves extension evaluations (e.g., if consumers were told the work boots would have leather uppers similar to those used in the tennis shoes). When the parent brand and the extension only share non-product associations and the parent brand image is product related, consumers often make negative inferences on the basis of existing associations (e.g., a tennis shoe with an image for durability attempting to extend to swimsuits can be seen as unfashionable). In this case, providing information that established an explanatory link on an entirely new, "reassuring" association—an "elaborational" communication strategy—improves extension evaluations (e.g., if consumers are told that the swimsuits would be similar in "fashionability" to the tennis shoes). They conclude that the most effective communication strategy for extensions appears to be one which recognizes the type of information that is already salient for the brand in the minds of consumers when they first considered the proposed extension and highlights additional information that would otherwise be overlooked or misinterpreted (see also Chakravarti, MacInnis, and Nakamoto 1990).

Lane (2000) finds that repetition of an ad that evoked primarily benefit brand associations can overcome negative perceptions of a highly incongruent brand extension. Moreover, for moderately incongruent brand extensions, even ads that evoke peripheral brand associations (e.g., brand packaging or character) can improve negative extension perceptions with sufficient repetition. Process measures reveal that, as a result of multiple exposures to ads for incongruent extensions, positive extension thoughts and thoughts of extension consistency eventually overcome the initial negative thoughts of inconsistency. In a somewhat similar vein, Barone, Miniard, and Romeo (2000) experimentally demonstrate that positive mood for consumers enhances evaluations of extensions viewed as moderately similar to (as opposed to very similar or dissimilar to) a favorably evaluated core brand. These effects of mood are found to be mediated by perceptions of the similarity between the core brand and the extension as well as the perceived competency of the marketer in producing the extension.

Finally, research explores several other aspects of extension marketing programs. Keller and Sood (2001a) find that "branding effects" in terms of inferences based on parent brand knowledge operate both in the absence and presence of product experience with an extension, although they are less pronounced with experience or, in the case of an unambiguous negative experience, even disappear. In considering the effects of retailer displays, Buchanan, Simmons, and Bickart (1999) find that evaluations of a "high equity" brand can be diminished by an unfamiliar competitive brand when a mixed display structure (where brands are interspersed among each other) leads consumers to believe that the competitive brand is diagnostic for judging the high equity brand and the competitive brand is given precedence over the high equity brand and is lower priced.

In conclusion, prior research provides a very comprehensive overview as to the factors affecting brand extension success as well as how brand extensions affect the parent brand. Next, we examine how brands can borrow or "leverage" equity for their products through branding strategies and brand alliances.

Leveraging Brand Equity: Branding Strategies and Brand Alliances

Branding Strategies

Brand strategies concern how brand elements such as brand name are employed across the products of a firm. LaForet and Saunders (1994) conduct a content analysis of the branding strategies adopted by 20 key brands sold by each of 20 of the biggest suppliers of grocery products to Tesco and Sainsbury's, Britain's two leading grocery chains. They find a variety of approaches that use common and/or distinct brands in different ways across the products sold by the firms (see also LaForet and Saunders 1999).

Sub-branding   One frequently employed branding strategy, sub-branding—whereby an existing name is combined with a new name to brand new products—has received some research attention. Prior research shows that a sub-branding strategy can enhance extension evaluations, especially if the extension is more removed from the product category and less similar in fit (Keller and Sood 2001a; Milberg, Park, and McCarthy 1997; Sheinin 1998). Moreover, it has been shown that a sub-brand can also protect the parent brand from unwanted negative feedback (Milberg, Park, and McCarthy 1997; Janiszewski and van Osselaer 2000; Kirmani, Sood, and Bridges 1999), but only if the sub-brand consists of a meaningful individual brand that precedes the family brand (e.g., Courtyard by Marriott) (Keller and Sood 2001b). Thus, it appears that the relative prominence of the brand elements determines which element(s) becomes the primary one(s) and which element(s) becomes the secondary one(s) (see also Park, Jun, and Shocker 1996).

Wänke, Bless, and Schwarz (1998) show how sub-branding strategy could help to set consumer expectations. Experimentally, a new compact car manufactured by a sports car company that has existing sports cars branded Winston Silverhawk, Winston Silverpride, and Winston Silverstar receives a more sports-car-typical evaluation when its name reflects the continuation (Winston Silverray) rather than the discontinuation of previous models (Winston Miranda). The lower evaluation created by the name discontinuation strategy is more pronounced for non-experts than experts.

In an econometric study of "twin automobiles" (i.e., made in the same plant with essentially the same physical attributes but different names, such as Ford Motor Company's Ford Thunderbird and Mercury Cougar), Sullivan (1998) finds that twins are not perceived as perfect substitutes given that their relative prices differ. Most importantly, parent brand quality reputation affects the relative prices of the twin pairs. Specifically, the average (mean) quality of the parent line increases the demand for used cars sold under the parent brand name.

Branded Variants   Bergen, Dutta, and Shugan (1996) study branded variants, the various models that manufacturers offer different retailers (see also Shugan 1989). They argue that as the number of branded variants increases, consumers' cost of shopping for a branded product across stores increases, leading to less shopping across stores. Because reduced shopping implies reduced competition, they reason that retailers should be more inclined to carry the branded product and provide greater retail service support. An empirical examination with data from three retailers across 14 product categories supports these notions.

Brand Alliances

Brand alliances occur when two brands are combined in some way as part of a product or as part of the marketing program (Rao 1997; Rao, Qu, and Ruekert 1999; Shocker, Srivastava, and Ruekert 1994). Prior research on brand alliances has explored the effects of three forms: co-branding, ingredient branding strategies, and advertising alliances.

Co-branding Park, Jun, and Shocker (1996) compare co-brands to "conceptual combinations" in psychology. Experimentally, they explore the different ways that Godiva (associated with expensive, high calorie boxed chocolates) and Slim-Fast (associated with inexpensive, low calorie diet food) could introduce a chocolate cake mix separately or together through a co-brand. The findings indicate that a co-branded brand extension that combines two brands with complementary attribute levels appears to have a better attribute profile in the minds of consumers than either a direct extension of the dominant brand or an extension that consists of two highly favorable—but not complementary—brands. Consistent with the conceptual combination literature, they also find that consumers' impressions of the co-branded concept are driven more by the header brand (e.g., Slim-Fast chocolate cake mix by Godiva was seen as lower calorie than if the product was called Godiva chocolate cake mix by Slim-Fast; the reverse was true for associations of richness and luxury). Relatedly, they also found that consumers' impressions of Slim-Fast after exposure to the co-branded concept are more likely to change when it is the header brand than when it is the modifier brand. Their findings show how carefully selected brands can be combined to overcome potential problems of negatively correlated attributes (e.g., rich taste and low calories).

Simonin and Ruth (1998) find that consumers' attitudes toward a brand alliance can influence subsequent impressions of each partner's brands (i.e., such that spillover effects exist), but these effects also depend on other factors such as product "fit" or compatibility and brand "fit" or image congruity. Brands less familiar than their partners contribute less to an alliance but experience stronger spillover effects than their more familiar partners. Relatedly, Voss and Tansuhaj (1999) find that consumer evaluations of an unknown brand from another country are more positive when a well-known domestic brand is used in an alliance.

Finally, Levin and Levin (2000) explore the effects of dual branding which they defined as a marketing strategy in which two brands (usually restaurants) share the same facilities while providing consumers with the opportunity to use either one or both brands. They found that when two brands are linked through a dual-branding arrangement and both brands are described by the same set of attributes, the effect of dual branding is to reduce or eliminate the contrast effects. When two brands are linked through a dual-branding arrangement and the target brand is less well specified than the context brand, then the effect of dual branding is to increase assimilation effects.

Ingredient Branding   A special case of co-branding is ingredient branding which involves creating brand equity for materials, components, parts, etc. that are necessarily contained within other branded products (Norris 1992; McCarthy and Norris 1999). Carpenter, Glazer, and Nakamoto (1994) find that the inclusion of a branded attribute (e.g., "Alpine Class" fill for a down jacket) significantly impacts consumer choices *even when consumers are explicitly told that the attribute is not relevant to their choice.* Subjects evidently infer certain quality characteristics as a result of the branded ingredient. Brown and Carpenter (2000) offer a reason-based account for the trivial attributes effect and show that the effect will depend on the choice context involved. Finally, Broniarczyk and Gershoff (2001) show that the effect of trivial differentiation is more pronounced with strong brands.

Desai and Keller (2002) conduct a laboratory experiment to consider how ingredient branding affects consumer acceptance of an initial line extension, as well as the ability of the brand to introduce future category extensions. Two particular types of line extensions, defined as brand expansions, are studied: *slot filler expansions,* where the level of one existing product attribute changes (e.g., a new type of scent in Tide detergent) and *new attribute expansions,* where an entirely new attribute or characteristic is added to the product (e.g., cough relief liquid added to LifeSavers candy). Two types of ingredient branding strategies are examined by branding the target-attribute ingredient for the brand expansion with either a new name as a *self-branded ingredient* (e.g., Tide with its own EverFresh scented bath soap) or an established, well-respected name as a *co-branded ingredient* (e.g., Tide with Irish Spring scented bath soap). The results indicate that with slot filler expansions, although a co-branded ingredient facilitates initial expansion acceptance, a self-branded ingredient leads to more favorable subsequent extension evaluations. (See also Janiszewski and van Osselaer 2000.) With more dissimilar new attribute expansions, however, a co-branded ingredient leads to more favorable evaluations of both the initial expansion and the subsequent extension.

Finally, Venkatesh and Mahajan (1997) derive an analytical model based on bundling and reservation price notions to help formulate optimal pricing and partner selection decisions for branded components. In an experimental application in the context of a university computer store selling "486 class" laptop computers, they show that at the bundle level, an all-brand Compaq PC with Intel 486 commands a clear price premium over other alternatives. The relative brand "strength" of the Intel brand, however, is shown to be stronger than that of the Compaq brand.

Advertising Alliances   In advertising alliances, two brands from different product categories are featured together in an ad, such as when Kellogg and Tropicana jointly sponsored an ad showing their products used together at breakfast. Samu, Krishnan, and Smith (1999) show that the effectiveness of such alliances for new product introductions depends on the interactive effects of three factors: the degree of complementarity between the featured products, the type of differentiation strategy (common versus unique advertised attributes with respect to the product category), and the type of ad processing (top-down or bottom-up) that an ad evokes (e.g., explicitness of ad headline).

Conclusions and Future Prospects

Before considering future research opportunities, it is worthwhile to take stock of progress thus far and consider the generalizations suggested by the research reviewed.

Summary Observations

Prior research has convincingly demonstrated the power of brands. Branding effects are pervasive, and the effects of virtually any marketing activity seem to be conditioned or qualified by the nature of the brands involved. In particular, consumer response to a product and its prices, advertising, promotions, and other aspects of the marketing program are shown to depend on the specific brands in question.

In examining how these branding effects are manifested, essentially all the theoretical approaches interpret them in terms of consumer knowledge about the brand and how that knowledge affects consumer behavior. The particular dimensions or aspects of brand knowledge that drive these differences in consumer response vary, however, by theoretical account and by the particular problem being investigated.

Some research has concentrated on the brand itself, e.g., the brand name or logo, and has shown that these elements can clearly contribute to brand equity by helping to convey product meaning to the consumer. Research has also provided theoretical and empirical insights into brand "intangibles," exploring concepts such as brand personality, experiences, relationships, and communities. This research shows how brand intangibles help make a brand more meaningful and relevant to consumers, creating stronger brand ties as a result. At a corporate brand level, researchers also show that corporate brands can have a broad set of associations that can facilitate product acceptance.

The most heavily researched area in branding is brand extensions. A key moderator of how consumers evaluate consumer evaluations of brand extensions is "fit": if a brand introduces an extension that is seen as closely related or similar in fit to the brand category, then consumers can easily transfer their existing attitudes about the parent brand to the extension. A successful extension not only contributes to the parent brand image but also enables a brand to be extended even farther. In general, unsuccessful extensions in dissimilar product categories do not affect evaluations of the parent brand, and unsuccessful extensions do not necessarily prevent a company from "retrenching" and later introducing a more similar extension.

Finally, research explores brand strategies and alliances, and how different combinations of brand names—those belonging to the company or to other companies—impact consumer response, and can improve product evaluations.

In conclusion, since brand knowledge plays a primary role in branding effects, however, it should be noted that branding effects are highly dependent on the context involved. Highlighting brand-related information can activate certain brand associations and not others in a manner to produce different outcomes. This differential accessibility may be a result of the cues in the marketing environment from the marketing program or through other means. Branding effects can thus be surprisingly complex. Moreover, brands themselves are inherently complex: brand names, logos, symbols, slogans, etc. have multiple dimensions, each with differential effects on consumer behavior.

Given the complexity and number of input and outcome variables, it is not surprising that brand management challenges can be thorny. Only by understanding the totality of the possible antecedents and consequences of brand marketing activity and the possible mechanisms involved can proper analysis be conducted and decisions executed.

Future Research

Although there has been much progress in the field, a number of important research priorities suggest that branding will be a fertile area for research for years to come (see Shocker, Srivastava, and Ruekert [1994] for an historical overview of branding progress and research agenda, as well as Berthon, Hulbert, and Pitt [1999]). The observations above suggest a broad research agenda for branding and brand management research, as follows:

Deeper, More Integrated Branding Research

Marketing has become increasingly complex as more ways to communicate with consumers, distribute products, etc. are being adopted by leading-edge firms. As a consequence, to provide greater managerial insight and guidance, there must be more sophisticated conceptual approaches to branding as well as correspondingly more varied and detailed measures of branding effects. These research imperatives should address the following three areas:

New Conceptual Models of Brand Equity   More fully articulated models of brand equity that provide greater expository detail and aid managers across a broad range of decision settings are needed. In addition, more parsimonious representations of such models will facilitate their applicability and use. Models that provide a more complete articulation of brand knowledge are especially needed, and more work needs to be done to better conceptualize "brand intangibles." There is much opportunity for multidisciplinary work that relies on complementary theoretical approaches and perspectives.

Better "Brand Metrics" and More Insightful Measures of Brand Equity
More insightful, diagnostic measures of branding phenomena are needed. This should involve multiple methods and measures, as decision makers require different types of information. For practicing managers, it is important to develop measures that directly relate marketing activity to actual brand performance. For senior management, it is important to develop highly reliable brand valuation techniques and means of assessing returns on brand investments. Of critical importance in this regard is achieving a better understanding of the value and contribution of brands in joint branding contexts and arrangements, whether with another brand, a person, an event, etc.

Effects of Marketing Activities As new alternative marketing approaches supplement more traditional strategies and tactics—especially in terms of communication and distribution—it will be important to fully understand their effects on consumers and optimal design and implementation. In addition, there is a critical need to understand how these different marketing activities should best be assembled as part of the marketing program. The advantages and disadvantages of different marketing activities and their potential interactions should be clarified so that they can be properly "mixed and matched" and integrated so that the whole is "greater than the sum of the parts."

Broader Branding Research

It is important that branding research take a broad perspective. In particular, branding research should take a strong internal branding point of view and consider the role of employees and other individuals inside the company in building and managing brand equity. However, since it is increasingly more difficult for brands to "go it alone" in the marketplace, it will also be important to take a strong external point of view and consider how brands can "borrow" equity in various ways. This suggests two additional lines of research.

Organizational, "Internal" Branding Issues A relatively neglected area of branding is prescriptive analyses of how different firms should best be organized for brand management. Additionally, more insight is needed into how to align brand management within the organization with those efforts directed to existing or prospective customers outside the organization.

How Meaning "Transfers" to and from Brands As brands are often linked with other entities—people, places, companies, brands, events—it is important to understand how knowledge about these other entities impacts brand knowledge. In what ways do the images of country-of-origin or country-of-brand, celebrity spokespeople, retail store, etc. change or supplement the brand image? At the same time, it is important to understand how the meaning of a brand transfers to other brands, products, etc.

More Relevant Branding Research

As branding is applied in more and more different settings, brand theory and best practice guidelines must be refined to reflect the unique realities of those settings. This suggests a final area for future research:

More Refined Models for Specific Application Areas of Branding The similarities and differences in branding for different types of application areas should receive greater research attention. One priority area of study is "virtual" branding and how brands should be built on the Internet. In general, researchers must seek to answer the question, How broadly applicable are the guidelines that emerge from academic research? Which principles are valid and which ones need to be modified or supplemented in some way?

One challenge in pursuing research in this area, as well as the other areas outlined above, is to achieve the necessary rigor to satisfy the highest academic standards while also achieving the necessary relevance to satisfy the most demanding industry practitioners.

Notes

1. A number of books, conferences (e.g., see summaries from the Marketing Science Institute and the Advertising Research Foundation), journals (*Journal of Brand Management*), and special issues of journals (*Journal of Marketing*, May 1994) have been devoted to the topic of branding in recent years.
2. Some early, seminal research of special note includes Allison and Uhl (1964), Dichter (1964), Gardner and Levy (1955), Haire (1950), and Levy (1959).

References

Aaker, David A. (1991), *Managing Brand Equity.* New York, N.Y.: Free Press.

Aaker, David A. (1994), "The Saturn Story: Building a Brand." *California Managment Review* 36 (2), 114-33.

Aaker, David A. (1996), *Building Strong Brands.* New York, N.Y.: Free Press.

Aaker, David A. (1997), "Should You Take Your Brand to Where the Action Is?" *Harvard Business Review* (September/October), 135–43.

Aaker, David A., and Robert Jacobson (1994), "The Financial Information Content of Perceived Quality." *Journal of Marketing Research* 31 (May), 191–201.

Aaker, David A., and Robert Jacobson (2001), "The Value Relevance of Brand Attitude in High-Technology Markets." *Journal of Marketing Research* 38 (November), 485–93.

Aaker, David A., and Erich Joachimsthaler (1999), "The Lure of Global Branding." *Harvard Business Review* (November/December), 137–44.

Aaker, David A., and Erich Joachimsthaler (2000), *Brand Leadership: Building Assets in an Information Economy.* New York, N.Y.: Free Press.

Aaker, David A., and Kevin Lane Keller (1990), "Consumer Evaluations of Brand Extensions." *Journal of Marketing* 54 (1) (January), 27–41.

Aaker, Jennifer L. (1997), "Dimensions of Brand Personality." *Journal of Marketing Research* 34 (August), 347–56.

Aaker, Jennifer L. (1999), "The Malleable Self: The Role of Self-Expression in Persuasion." *Journal of Marketing Research* 36 (February), 45–7.

Aaker, Jennifer L., Verónica Benet-Martínez, and Jordi Garolera Berrocal (2001), "Consumption Symbols as Carriers of Culture: A Study of Japanese and Spanish Brand Personality Constructs." *Journal of Personality and Psychology* 81 (3), 492–508.

Aaker, Jennifer L., Susan Fournier, and S. A. Brasel (2001), "Charting the Development of Consumer-Brand Relationships." Stanford, Calif.: Stanford University, Working Paper.

Achenreiner, Gwen B., and Deborah Roedder John (2002), "The Meaning of Brand Names to Children: A Developmental Investigation." *Journal of Consumer Psychology,* forthcoming.

Agrawal, Deepak (1996), "Effect of Brand Loyalty on Advertising and Trade Promotions: A Game Theoretic Analysis with Empirical Evidence." *Marketing Science* 15 (1), 86–108.

Ahluwalia, Rohini, Robert E. Burnkrant, and H. R. Unnava (2000), "Consumer Response to Negative Publicity: The Moderating Role of Commitment." *Journal of Marketing Research* 37 (May), 203–14.

Ahluwalia, Rohini, and Zeynep Gürhan-Canli (2000), "The Effects of Extensions on the Family Brand Name: An Accessibility-Diagnosticity Perspective." *Journal of Consumer Research* 27 (3) (December), 371–81.

Allenby, Greg M., and Peter E. Rossi (1991), "Quality Perceptions and Asymmetric Switching Between Brands." *Marketing Science* 10 (3), 185–204.

Allison, R. I., and K. P. Uhl (1964), "Brand Identification and Perception." *Journal of Marketing Research* 1 (August), 80–5.

Ambler, Tim (2000), *Marketing and the Bottom Line*. London, U.K.: Pearson Education.

Andrews, Jonlee, and George S. Low (1998), "New But Not Improved: Factors That Affect the Development of Meaningful Line Extensions." Cambridge, Mass.: Marketing Science Institute, Report No. 98-124.

Baldinger, Allan L., and Joel Rubinson (1997), "In Search of the Holy Grail: A Rejoinder." *Journal of Advertising Research* 37 (1), 18–20.

Barich, Howard, and Philip Kotler (1991), "A Framework for Marketing Image Management." *Sloan Management Review* 32 (2), 94–104.

Barone, Michael J., Paul W. Miniard, and Jean B. Romeo (2000), "The Influence of Positive Mood on Brand Extension Evaluations." *Journal of Consumer Research* 26 (4), 386–400.

Barth, Mary E., Michael Clement, George Foster, and Ron Kasznik (1998), "Brand Values and Capital Market Valuation." *Review of Accounting Studies* 3, 41–68.

Barwise, T. Patrick, Chris Higson, Andrew Likierman, and Paul Marsh (1989), *Accounting for Brands*. London, U.K.: London Business School, ICAEW.

Belch, George E. (1981), "An Examination of Comparative and Noncomparative Television Commercials: The Effects of Claim Variation and Repetition on Cognitive Response and Message Acceptance." *Journal of Marketing Research* 18 (August), 333–49.

Bello, Daniel C., and Morris B. Holbrook (1995), "Does an Absence of Brand Equity Generalize across Product Classes?" *Journal of Business Research* 34 (2), 125–31.

Bemmaor, Albert C., and Dominique Mouchoux (1991), "Measuring the Short-Term Effect of In-Store Promotion and Retail Advertising on Brand Sales: A Factorial Experiment." *Journal of Marketing Research* 28 (May), 202–14.

Bergen, Mark, Shantanu Dutta, and Steven M. Shugan (1996), "Branded Variants: A Retail Perspective." *Journal of Marketing Research* 33 (February), 9–21.

Berthon, Pierre, James M. Hulbert, and Leyland F. Pitt (1999), "Brand Management Prognostications." *Sloan Management Review* 40 (2), 53–65.

Bhattacharya, C. B., and Leonard M. Lodish (2000), "Towards a System for Monitoring Brand Health from Store Scanner Data." Cambridge, Mass.: Marketing Science Institute, Report No. 00-111.

Biehal, Gabriel J., and Daniel A. Sheinin (1998), "Managing the Brand in a Corporate Advertising Environment: A Decision-Making Framework for Brand Managers." *Journal of Advertising* 27 (2), 99–110.

Bijmolt, T. H. A., M. Wedel, R. G. M. Pieters, and Wayne S. DeSarbo (1998), "Judgments of Brand Similarity." *International Journal of Research in Marketing* 15 (3), 249–68.

Blattberg, Robert C., and Kenneth J. Wisniewski (1989), "Price-Induced Patterns of Competition." *Marketing Science* 8 (4), 291–309.

Bong, N. W., Roger Marshall, and Kevin Lane Keller (1999), "Measuring Brand Power: Validating a Model for Optimizing Brand Equity." *Journal of Product and Brand Management* 8 (3), 170–84.

Bottomley, Paul A., and Stephen J. S. Holden (2001), "Do We Really Know How Consumers Evaluate Brand Extensions? Empirical Generalizations Based on Secondary Analysis of Eight Studies." *Journal of Marketing Research* 38 (November), 494–500.

Boulding, William, Eunkyu Lee, and Richard Staelin (1994), "Mastering the Marketing Mix: Do Advertising, Promotion, and Sales Force Activities Lead to Differentiation?" *Journal of Marketing Research* 31 (May), 159–72.

Boush, David M. (1993), "How Advertising Slogans Can Prime Evaluations of Brand Extensions." *Psychology & Marketing* 10 (1), 67–78.

Boush, David M. (1997), "Brand Name Effects on Interproduct Similarity Judgments." *Marketing Letters* 8 (4), 419–27.

Boush, David M., and Barbara Loken (1991), "A Process-Tracing Study of Brand Extension Evaluation." *Journal of Marketing Research* 28 (February), 16–28.

Boush, David, Shannon Shipp, Barbara Loken, Esra Gencturk, Susan Crockett, Ellen Kennedy, Bettie Minshall, Dennis Misurell, Linda Rochford, and Jon Strobel (1987), "Affect Generalization to Similar and Dissimilar Brand Extensions." *Psychology & Marketing* 4 (3), 225–37.

Bridges, Sheri, Kevin Lane Keller, and Sanjay Sood (2000), "Explanatory Links and the Perceived Fit of Brand Extensions: The Role of Dominant Parent Brand Associations and Communication Strategies." *Journal of Advertising* 29 (4), 1–11.

Bristol, Terry (1996), "Consumers' Beliefs Resulting from Conceptual Combinations: Conjunctive Inferences about Brand Extensions." *Psychology & Marketing* 13 (6), 571–89.

Broniarczyk, Susan M., and Joseph W. Alba (1994), "The Importance of the Brand in Brand Extension." *Journal of Marketing Research* 31 (May), 214–28.

Broniarczyk, Susan M., and Andrew D. Gershoff (2001), "The Reciprocal Effects of Brand Equity and Trivial Differentiation." Austin, Tex.: University of Texas, Working Paper.

Brown, Christina L., and Gregory S. Carpenter (2000), "Why Is the Trivial Important? A Reasons-Based Account for the Effects of Trivial Attributes on Choice." *Journal of Consumer Research* 26 (4), 372–85.

Brown, Steven P., and Douglas M. Stayman (1992), "Antecedents and Consequences of Attitude toward the Ad: A Meta-analysis." *Journal of Consumer Research* 19 (1), 34–51.

Brown, Thomas J. (1998), "Corporate Associations in Marketing: Antecedents and Consequences." *Corporate Reputation Review* 1 (3), 215–33.

Brown, Tom J., and Peter Dacin (1997), "The Company and the Product: Corporate Associations and Consumer Product Responses." *Journal of Marketing* 61 (1) (January), 68–84.

Buchanan, Lauranne, Carolyn J. Simmons, and Barbara A. Bickart (1999), "Brand Equity Dilution: Retailer Display and Context Brand Effects." *Journal of Marketing Research* 36 (August), 345–55.

Bucklin, Randolph E., Sunil Gupta, and Sangman Han (1995), "Brand's Eye View of Response Segmentation in Consumer Brand Choice Behavior." *Journal of Marketing Research* 32 (February), 66–74.

Calder, Bobby J., and Brian Sternthal (1980), "Television Commercial Wearout: An Information Processing View." *Journal of Marketing Research* 27 (May), 173–86.

Campbell, Margaret, and Kevin Lane Keller (2002), "The Moderating Effect of Brand Knowledge on Ad Repetition Effects." Boulder, Colo.: University of Colorado, Boulder, Working Paper.

Carpenter, Gregory S., Rashi Glazer, and Kent Nakamoto (1994), "Meaningful Brands from Meaningless Differentiation: The Dependence on Irrelevant Attributes." *Journal of Marketing Research* 31 (August), 339–50.

Chakravarti, Dipankar, Deborah MacInnis, and Kent Nakamoto (1990), "Product Category Perceptions, Elaborative Processing and Brand Name Extension Strategies." In *Advances in Consumer Research,* vol. 17, eds. Marvin Goldberg, Gerald Gorn and Richard Pollay, 910-6. Provo, Utah: Association for Consumer Research.

Chattopadhyay, Amitava, and Kunal Basu (1990), "Humor in Advertising: The Moderating Role of Prior Brand Evaluation." *Journal of Marketing Research* 27 (November), 466–76.

Chaudhuri, Arjun (1999), "Does Brand Loyalty Mediate Brand Equity Outcomes?" *Journal of Marketing Theory and Practice* 7 (2) (Spring), 136–46.

Chaudhuri, Arjun, and Morris B. Holbrook (2001), "The Chain of Effects from Brand Trust and Brand Affect to Brand Performance: The Role of Brand Loyalty." *Journal of Marketing* 65 (2) (April), 81–93.

Cohen, Dorothy (1986), "Trademark Strategy." *Journal of Marketing* 50 (1) (January), 61–74.

Cohen, Dorothy (1991), "Trademark Strategy Revisited." *Journal of Marketing* 55 (3) (July), 46–59.

Cohen, Morris A., Jehoshua Eliashberg, and Teck H. Ho (1997), "An Anatomy of a Decision-Support System for Developing and Launching Line Extensions." *Journal of Marketing Research* 34 (February), 117–29.

Dacin, Peter, and Daniel C. Smith (1994), "The Effect of Brand Portfolio Characteristics on Consumer Evaluations of Brand Extensions." *Journal of Marketing Research* 31 (May), 229–42.

Dawar, Niraj (1996), "Extensions of Broad Brands: The Role of Retrieval in Evaluations of Fit." *Journal of Consumer Psychology* 5 (2), 189–207.

Dawar, Niraj, and Paul F. Anderson (1994), "The Effects of Order and Direction on Multiple Brand Extensions." *Journal of Business Research* 30, 119–29.

Dawar, Niraj, and Madan M. Pillutla (2000), "Impact of Product-Harm Crises on Brand Equity: The Moderating Role of Consumer Expectations." *Journal of Marketing Research* 37 (May), 215–26.

Day, George S., and Terry Deutscher (1982), "Attitudinal Predictions of Choices of Major Appliance Brands." *Journal of Marketing Research* 19 (May), 192–8.

DeGraba, Patrick, and Mary W. Sullivan (1995), "Spillover Effects, Cost Savings, R&D and the Use of Brand Extensions." *International Journal of Industrial Organization* 13 (2), 229–48.

Desai, Kalpesh Kaushik, and Kevin Lane Keller (2002), "The Effects of Ingredient Branding Strategies on Host Brand Extendibility." *Journal of Marketing* 66 (1) (January), 73–93.

Dhar, Ravi, and Itamar Simonson (1992), "The Effect of the Focus of Comparison on Consumer Preferences." *Journal of Marketing Research* 29 (November), 430–40.

Dichter, Ernest (1964), *Handbook of Consumer Motivations.* New York, N.Y.: McGraw-Hill.

Dillon, William R., Thomas J. Madden, Amna Kirmani, and Soumen Mukherjee (2001), "Understanding What's in a Brand Rating: A Model for Assessing Brand and Attribute Effects and Their Relationship to Brand Equity." *Journal of Marketing Research* 38 (November), 415–29.

Dodds, William B., Kent B. Monroe, and Dhruv Grewal (1991), "Effects of Price, Brand, and Store Information on Buyers' Product Evaluations." *Journal of Marketing Research* 28 (August), 307–19.

Doeden, D. L. (1981), "How to Select a Brand Name." *Marketing Communications* (November), 58–61.

Dowling, Grahame R. (1994), *Corporate Reputations.* London, U.K.: Kogan Page.

Drumwright, Minette (1996), "Company Advertising with a Social Dimension: The Role of Noneconomic Criteria." *Journal of Marketing* 60 (4) (October), 71–87.

Duke, Charles R. (1995), "Exploratory Comparisons of Alternative Memory Measures for Brand Name." *Psychology & Marketing* 12 (1), 19–36.

Dyson, Paul, Andy Farr, and Nigel Hollis (1997), "What Does the Marketing Team Need, Description or Prescription? A Response to Comments by Andrew Ehrenberg." *Journal of Advertising Research* 37 (1), 13–7.

Ehrenberg, Andrew S. C. (1997), "In Search of Holy Grails: Two Comments." *Journal of Advertising Research* 37 (1), 9–12.

Ehrenberg, Andrew S. C., Neil Barnard, and John Scriven (1997), "Differentiation or Salience." *Journal of Advertising Research* 37 (6), 82–91.

Ehrenberg, Andrew S. C., Gerald Goodhardt, and T. Patrick Barwise (1990), "Double Jeopardy Revisited." *Journal of Marketing* 54 (3) (July), 82–91.

Epstein, Marc J., and Robert A. Westbrook (2001), "Linking Actions to Profits in Strategic Decision Making." *Sloan Management Review* 42 (3), 39–49.

Erdem, Tülin (1998a), "An Empirical Analysis of Umbrella Branding." *Journal of Marketing Research* 35 (August), 339–51.

Erdem, Tülin (1998b), "Brand Equity as a Signaling Phenomenon." *Journal of Consumer Psychology* 7 (2), 131–57.

Fader, Peter S., and David C. Schmittlein (1993), "Excess Behavioral Loyalty for High-Share Brands: Deviations from the Dirichlet Model for Repeat Purchasing." *Journal of Marketing Research* 30 (November), 478–93.

Farquhar, Peter H. (1989), "Managing Brand Equity." *Marketing Research* 1 (September), 24–33.

Farquhar, Peter H., J. Y. Han, Paul M. Herr, and Yuji Ijiri (1992), "Strategies for Leveraging Master Brands." *Marketing Research* 4 (September), 32–43.

Farquhar, Peter H., and P. M. Herr (1992), "The Dual Structure of Brand Associations." In *Brand Equity and Advertising: Advertising's Role in Building Strong Brands,* eds. David A. Aaker and Alexander L. Biel, 263–77. Hillsdale, N.J.: Lawrence Erlbaum Associates.

Feinberg, Fred M., Barbara E. Kahn, and Leigh McAlister (1992), "Market Share Response When Consumers Seek Variety." *Journal of Marketing Research* 29 (May), 227–37.

Feldwick, Paul (1996), "Do We Really Need 'Brand Equity'?" *The Journal of Brand Management* 4 (1), 9–28.

Fournier, Susan (1998), "Consumers and Their Brands: Developing Relationship Theory in Consumer Research." *Journal of Consumer Research* 24 (4), 343–73.

Fournier, Susan M. (2000), "Dimensioning Brand Relationships Using Brand Relationship Quality." Presentation at the Association for Consumer Research annual conference, Salt Lake City, Utah, October.

Fournier, Susan M., Susan Dobscha, and David Glen Mick (1998), "Preventing the Premature Death of Relationship Marketing." *Harvard Business Review* (January–February), 42–51.

Fournier, Susan M., and Julie L. Yao (1997), "Reviving Brand Loyalty: A Reconceptualization within the Framework of Consumer-Brand Relationships." *International Journal of Research in Marketing* 14 (5), 451–72.

Foxman, Ellen R., Paul W. Berger, and Joseph A. Cote (1992), "Consumer Brand Confusion: A Conceptual Framework." *Psychology & Marketing* 9 (2), 123–41.

Gardner, Burleigh B., and Sydney J. Levy (1955), "The Product and the Brand." *Harvard Business Review* (March–April), 33–9.

Golder, Peter N. (2000), "Historical Method in Marketing Research with New Evidence on Long-Term Stability." *Journal of Marketing Research* 37 (May), 156–72.

Graeff, Timothy R. (1996), "Image Congruence Effects on Product Evaluations: The Role of Self-Monitoring and Public/Private Consumption." *Psychology & Marketing* 13 (5), 481–99.

Graeff, Timoth R. (1997), "Consumption Situations and the Effects of Brand Image on Consumers' Brand Evaluations." *Psychology & Marketing* 14 (1), 49–70.

Grover, Rajiv, and V. Srinivasan (1992), "Evaluating the Multiple Effects of Retail Promotions on Brand Loyal and Brand Switching Segments." *Journal of Marketing Research* 29 (February), 76–89.

Gürhan-Canli, Zeynep, and Durairaj Maheswaran (1998), "The Effects of Extensions on Brand Name Dilution and Enhancement." *Journal of Marketing Research* 35 (November), 464–73.

Haire, Mason (1950), "Projective Techniques in Marketing Research." *Journal of Marketing* (April), 649–56.

Han, Jin K., and Bernd H. Schmitt (1997), "Product Category Dynamics and Corporate Identity in Brand Extensions: A Comparison of Hong Kong and U.S. Consumers." *Journal of International Marketing* 5 (1), 77–92.

Hardie, Bruce G. S., Leonard M. Lodish, James V. Kilmer, David R. Beatty, Paul W. Farris, Alexander L. Biel, Laura S. Wicke, John B. Balson, and David A. Aaker (1994), "The Logic of Product-Line Extensions." *Harvard Business Review* (November–December), 53–62.

Hartman, Cathy L., Linda L. Price, and Calvin P. Duncan (1990), "Consumer Evaluation of Franchise Extension Products: A Categorization Processing Perspective." In *Advances in Consumer Research* vol. 17, eds. Marvin Goldberg, Gerald Gorn, and Richard Pollay, 120-6. Provo, Utah: Association for Consumer Research.

Harvey, Michael, James T. Rothe, and Laurie A. Lucas (1998), "The 'Trade Dress' Controversy: A Case of Strategic Cross-Brand Cannibalization." *Journal of Marketing Theory and Practice* (Spring), 1–15.

Heath, Timothy B., S. Chatterjee, and Karen Russo (1990), "Using the Phonemes of Brand Names to Symbolize Brand Attributes." In *The AMA Educators' Proceedings: Enhancing Knowledge Development in Marketing,* eds. William Bearden and A. Parasuraman. Chicago, Ill.: American Marketing Association.

Heath, Timothy B., Michael S. McCarthy, and Sandra J. Milberg (2001), "New Brands Versus Brand Extensions, Attitudes Versus Choice: Experimental Evidence for Theory and Practice." *Marketing Letters* 12 (1) (February), 75–90.

Hem, Leif E., and N. M. Iverson (2001), "Context Effects in Brand Extensions: Implications for Evaluations." Bergen, Norway: Norwegian School of Economics and Business Administration, Working Paper.

Henderson, Geraldine R., Dawn Iacobucci, and Bobby J. Calder (1998), "Brand Diagnostics: Mapping Branding Effects Using Consumer Associative Networks." *European Journal of Operational Research* 111, 306–27.

Henderson, Pamela W. and Joseph A. Cote (1998), "Guidelines for Selecting or Modifying Logos." *Journal of Marketing* 62 (2) (April), 14–30.

Herr, Paul M., Peter H. Farquhar, and Russell H. Fazio (1996), "Impact of Dominance and Relatedness on Brand Extensions." *Journal of Consumer Psychology* 5 (2), 135–59.

Hoeffler, Stephen, and Kevin Lane Keller (2001), "The Marketing Advantages of Strong Brands." Chapel Hill, N.C.: University of North Carolina at Chapel Hill, Working Paper.

Holbrook, Morris B. (1992), "Product Quality, Attributes, and Brand Name as Determinants of Price: The Case of Consumer Electronics." *Marketing Letters* 3 (1), 71–83.

Hutchinson, J. Wesley, Kalyan Raman, and Murali K. Mantrala (1994), "Finding Choice Alternatives in Memory: Probability Models of Brand Name Recall." *Journal of Marketing Research* 31 (November), 441–61.

Janiszewski, Chris, and Tom Meyvis (2001), "Effects of Brand Logo Complexity, Repetition, and Spacing on Processing Fluency and Judgment." *Journal of Consumer Research* 28 (June), 18–32.

Janiszewski, Chris, and Stijn M. J. van Osselaer (2000), "A Connectionist Model of Brand-Quality Associations." *Journal of Marketing Research* 37 (August), 331–50.

Jap, Sandy D. (1993), "An Examination of the Effects of Multiple Brand Extensions on the Brand Concept." In *Advances in Consumer Research* vol. 20, eds. Leigh McAlister and Michael L. Rothschild, 607-11. Provo, Utah: Association for Consumer Research.

Joachimsthaler, Erich, and David A. Aaker (1997), "Building Brands without Mass Media." *Harvard Business Review* (January-February), 39-50.

John, Deborah Roedder, Barbara Loken, and Christopher Joiner (1998), "The Negative Impact of Extensions: Can Flagship Products Be Diluted?" *Journal of Marketing* 62 (1) (January), 19–32.

Joiner, Christopher, and Barbara Loken (1998), "The Inclusion Effect and Category-Based Induction: Theory and Application to Brand Categories." *Journal of Consumer Psychology* 7 (2), 101–29.

Journal of Advertising (1995), "Special Issue on Green Advertising."

Kamakura, Wagner A., and Gary J. Russell (1993), "Measuring Brand Value with Scanner Data." *International Journal of Research in Marketing* 10 (1), 9–22.

Kamins, Michael A., and Lawrence J. Marks (1991), "The Perception of Kosher as a Third Party Certification Claim in Advertising for Familiar and Unknown Brands." *Journal of Academy of Marketing Science* 19 (3) (Summer), 177–85.

Kanetkar, Vinay, Charles B. Weinberg, and Doyle L. Weiss (1992), "Price Sensitivity and Television Advertising Exposures: Some Empirical Findings." *Marketing Science* 11 (4) (Fall), 359–71.

Kapferer, Jean-Noël (1994), *Strategic Brand Management*. New York, N.Y.: Free Press.

Kapferer, Jean-Noël (1995), "Stealing Brand Equity: Measuring Perceptual Confusion Between National Brands and 'Copycat' Own-Label Products." *Marketing and Research Today* (May), 96–103.

Kardes, Frank R., and Chris T. Allen (1990), "Perceived Variability and Inferences about Brand Extensions." In *Advances in Consumer Research*, vol. 18, eds. Rebecca H. Holman and Michael R. Solomon, 392–8. Provo, Utah: Association for Consumer Research.

Keller, Kevin Lane (1993), "Conceptualizing, Measuring, and Managing Customer-Based Brand Equity." *Journal of Marketing* 57 (1) (January), 1–22.

Keller, Kevin Lane (1998), *Strategic Brand Management*. Upper Saddle River, N.J.: Prentice-Hall.

Keller, Kevin Lane (1999a), "Effective Long-Run Brand Management: Brand Reinforcement and Revitalization Strategies." *California Management Review* 41 (3), 102–24.

Keller, Kevin Lane (1999b), "Designing and Implementing Branding Strategies." *Journal of Brand Management* 6 (5), 315–31.

Keller, Kevin Lane (2000), "The Brand Report Card." *Harvard Business Review* (January/February), 147–57.

Keller, Kevin Lane (2001), "Building Customer-Based Brand Equity: A Blueprint for Creating Strong Brands." *Marketing Management* (July/August), 15–9.

Keller, Kevin Lane, and David A. Aaker (1992), "The Effects of Sequential Introduction of Brand Extensions." *Journal of Marketing Research* 29 (February), 35–50.

Keller, Kevin Lane, and David A. Aaker (1998), "Corporate-Level Marketing: The Impact of Credibility on a Company's Brand Extensions." *Corporate Reputation Review* 1 (August), 356–78.

Keller, Kevin Lane, Susan Heckler, and Michael J. Houston (1998), "The Effects of Brand Name Suggestiveness on Advertising Recall." *Journal of Marketing* 62 (1) (January), 48–57.

Keller, Kevin Lane, and Donald R. Lehmann (2002), "The Brand Value Chain: Optimizing Strategic and Financial Brand Performance." Hanover, N.H.: Dartmouth College, Working Paper.

Keller, Kevin Lane, and Sanjay Sood (2001a), "The Effects of Product Experience and Branding Strategies on Brand Evaluations." Los Angeles, Calif.: University of California at Los Angeles, Working Paper.

Keller, Kevin Lane, and Sanjay Sood (2001b), "The Effects of Alternative Sub-Branding Strategies on Consumer Brand Evaluations." Los Angeles, Calif.: University of California at Los Angeles, Working Paper.

Kent, Robert J., and Chris T. Allen (1994), "Competitive Interference Effects in Consumer Memory for Advertising: The Role of Brand Familiarity." *Journal of Marketing* 58 (3) (July), 97–105.

Kerin, Roger A., Gurumurthy Kalyanaram, and Daniel J. Howard (1996), "Product Hierarchy and Brand Strategy Influences on the Order of Entry Effect for Consumer Packaged Goods." *Journal of Product Innovation Management* 13 (1) (January), 21–34.

Kirmani, Amna, Sanjay Sood, and Sheri Bridges (1999), "The Ownership Effect in Consumer Responses to Brand Line Stretches." *Journal of Marketing* 63 (1) (January), 88–101.

Klink, Richard R. (2000), "Creating Brand Names with Meaning: The Use of Sound Symbolism." *Marketing Letters* 11 (1) (February), 5–20.

Klink, Richard R., and Daniel C. Smith (2001), "Threats to the External Validity of Brand Extension Research." *Journal of Marketing* 38 (August), 326–35.

Kohli, Chiranjeev, and Douglas LaBahn (1997), "Creating Effective Brand Names: A Study of the Naming Process." *Journal of Advertising Research* 37 (1), 67–75.

Kotler, Philip (2000), *Marketing Management.* Upper Saddle River, N.J.: Prentice-Hall.

Krishnamurthi, Lakshman, and S. P. Raj (1991), "An Empirical Analysis of the Relationship Between Brand Loyalty and Consumer Price Elasticity." *Marketing Science* 10 (2) (Spring), 172–83.

Krishnan, H. Shankar (1996), "Characteristics of Memory Associations: A Consumer-Based Brand Equity Perspective." *International Journal of Research in Marketing* 13 (4), 389–405.

Laczniak, Russell N., Thomas E. DeCarlo, and Sridhar N. Ramaswami (2001), "Consumers' Responses to Negative Word-of-Mouth Communication: An Attribution Theory Perspective." *Journal of Consumer Psychology* 11 (1), 57–73.

LaForet, Sylvia, and John Saunders (1994), "Managing Brand Portfolios: How the Leaders Do It." *Journal of Advertising Research* (September/October), 64–76.

LaForet, Sylvia, and John Saunders (1999), "Managing Brand Portfolios: Why Leaders Do What They Do." *Journal of Advertising Research* (January/February), 51–65.

Lal, Rajiv, and Chakravarthi Narasimhan (1996), "The Inverse Relationship Between Manufacturer and Retailer Margins: A Theory." *Marketing Science* 15 (2), 132–51.

Lane, Vicki R. (2000), "The Impact of Ad Repetition and Ad Content on Consumer Perceptions of Incongruent Extensions." *Journal of Marketing* 64 (4), 80–91.

Lane, Vicki R., and Robert Jacobson (1995), "Stock Market Reactions to Brand Extension Announcements: The Effects of Brand Attitude and Familiarity." *Journal of Marketing* 59 (1) (January), 63–77.

Lane, Vicki, and Robert Jacobson (1997), "The Reciprocal Impact of Brand Leveraging: Feedback Effects from Brand Extension Evaluation to Brand Evaluation." *Marketing Letters* 8 (3), 261–71.

Laroche, Michael, C. Kim, and Lianxi Zhou (1996), "Brand Familiarity and Confidence as Determinants of Purchase Intention: An Empirical Test in a Multiple Brand Context." *Journal of Business Research* 37 (2), 115–20.

Lassar, Walfried, Banwari Mittal, and Arun Sharma (1995), "Measuring Customer-Based Brand Equity." *Journal of Consumer Marketing* 12 (4), 11–9.

Leclerc, France, Bernd H. Schmitt, and Laurette Dubé (1994), "Foreign Branding and Its Effects on Product Perceptions and Attitudes." *Journal of Marketing Research* 31 (5), 263–70.

Lee, Moonkyu, Jonathan Lee, and Wagner A. Kamakura (1996), "Consumer Evaluations of Line Extensions: A Conjoint Approach." In *Advances in Consumer Research* vol. 23, eds. Kim P. Corfman and John G. Lynch, Jr., 289–95. Provo, Utah: Association for Consumer Research.

Levin, Irwin P., and Aron M. Levin (2000), "Modeling the Role of Brand Alliances in the Assimilation of Product Evaluations." *Journal of Consumer Psychology* 9 (1), 43–52.

Levy, Sydney J. (1959), "Symbols for Sale." *Harvard Business Review* 37 (March/April), 117–24.

Levy, Sydney J. (1999), *Brands, Consumers, Symbols, and Research: Sydney J. Levy on Marketing.* Thousand Oaks, Calif.: Sage Publications.

Loken, Barbara, and Deborah Roedder John (1993), "Diluting Brand Beliefs: When Do Brand Extensions Have a Negative Impact?" *Journal of Marketing* 57 (July) (3), 71–84.

Loken, Barbara, Ivan Ross, and Ross Hinkle (1986), "Consumer Confusion of 'Origin' and Brand Similarity Perceptions." *Journal of Public Policy and Marketing* 5, 195–211.

Machleit, Karen A., Chris T. Allen, and Thomas J. Madden (1993), "The Mature Brand and Brand Interest: An Alternative Consequence of Ad-Evoked Affect." *Journal of Marketing* 57 (4) (October), 72–82.

Mahajan, Vijay, Vithala Rao, and R. K. Srivastava (1994), "An Approach to Assess the Importance of Brand Equity in Acquisition Decisions." *Journal of Product Innovation Management* 11 (3), 221–35.

Martin, Ingrid M., and David W. Stewart (2001), "The Differential Impact of Goal Congruency on Attitudes, Intentions, and the Transfer of Brand Equity." *Journal of Marketing Research* 38 (November), 471–84.

McAlexander, James H., John W. Schouten, and Harold F. Koenig (2002), "Building Brand Community." *Journal of Marketing* 66 (January), 38–54.

McCarthy, Michael S., and Donald G. Norris (1999), "Improving Competitive Position Using Branded Ingredients." *Journal of Product & Brand Management* 8 (4), 267–85.

McCracken, Grant (1986), "Culture and Consumption: A Theoretical Account of the Structure and Movement of the Cultural Meaning of Consumer Goods." *Journal of Consumer Research* 13 (1) (June), 71–84.

McCracken, Grant (1993), "The Value of the Brand: An Anthropological Perspective." In *Brand Equity and Advertising: Advertising's Role in Building Strong Brands,* eds. David Aaker and Alexander Biel, 125–39. Hillsdale, N.J.: Lawrence Erlbaum Associates.

Menon, Ajay, and Anil Menon (1997), "Enviropreneurial Marketing Strategy: The Emergence of Corporate Environmentalism as Market Strategy." *Journal of Marketing* 61 (1) (January), 51–67.

Meyers-Levy, Joan (1989), "The Influence of a Brand Name's Association Set Size and Word Frequency on Brand Memory." *Journal of Consumer Research* 16 (September), 197–207.

Meyers-Levy, Joan, Therese A. Louie, and Mary T. Curren (1994), "How Does the Congruity of Brand Names Affect Evaluations of Brand Name Extensions?" *Journal of Applied Psychology* 79 (1), 46–53.

Milberg, Sandra J., C. Whan Park, and Michael S. McCarthy (1997), "Managing Negative Feedback Effects Associated with Brand Extensions: The Impact of Alternative Branding Strategies." *Journal of Consumer Psychology* 6 (2), 119–40.

Montgomery, Charles A., and Birger Wernerfelt (1992), "Risk Reduction and Umbrella Advertising." *Journal of Business* 65 (1), 31–50.

Montgomery, David B. (1975), "New Product Distribution—An Analysis of Supermarket Buyer Decisions." *Journal of Marketing Research* 12 (August), 255–64.

Morrin, Maureen (1999), "The Impact of Brand Extensions on Parent Brand Memory Structures and Retrieval Processes." *Journal of Marketing Research* 36 (4), 517–25.

Muniz, Albert M., Jr., and Thomas C. O'Guinn (2001), "Brand Community." *Journal of Consumer Research* 27 (4) (March), 412–32.

Muthukrishnan, A. V., and Barton A. Weitz (1990), "Role of Product Knowledge in Brand Extension." In *Advances in Consumer Research* vol. 18, eds. Rebecca H. Holman and Michael R. Solomon, 407–13. Provo, Utah: Association for Consumer Research.

Nguyen, L. T., and Deborah Roedder John (2001), "'Abercrombie & Fitch— That's Me:' Brand Names in Children's Self Concepts." Minneapolis, Minn.: University of Minnesota, Working Paper.

Norris, Donald G. (1992), "Ingredient Branding: A Strategy Option with Multiple Beneficiaries." *Journal of Consumer Marketing* 9 (Summer), 19–31.

Oakenfull, Gillian, and Betsy Gelb (1996), "Research-Based Advertising to Preserve Brand Equity but Avoid 'Genericide.'" *Journal of Advertising Research* (September/October), 65–72.

Pan, Y., and Bernd Schmitt (1996), "Language and Brand Attitudes: Impact of Script and Sound Matching in Chinese and English." *Journal of Consumer Psychology* 5 (3), 263–77.

Park, C. Whan, Bernard J. Jaworski, and Deborah J. MacInnis (1986), "Strategic Brand Concept-Image Management." *Journal of Marketing* 50 (4) (October), 135–45.

Park, C. Whan, Sung Youl Jun, and Allan D. Shocker (1996), "Composite Branding Alliances: An Investigation of Extension and Feedback Effects." *Journal of Marketing Research* 33 (November), 453–66.

Park, C. Whan, Sandra Milberg, and Robert Lawson (1991), "Evaluation of Brand Extensions: The Role of Product Feature Similarity and Brand Concept Consistency." *Journal of Consumer Research* 18 (2) (September), 185–93.

Park, Chan Su, and V. Srinivasan (1994), "A Survey-Based Method for Measuring and Understanding Brand Equity and its Extendibility." *Journal of Marketing Research* 31 (May), 271–88.

Pavia, Teresa M., and Janeen A. Costa (1993), "The Winning Number: Consumer Perceptions of Alpha-Numeric Brand Names." *Journal of Marketing* 57 (3) (July), 85–98.

Peterson, Robert A., and Ivan Ross (1972), "How to Name New Brands." *Journal of Advertising Research* 12 (6), 29–34.

Putsis, William P., Jr., and Barry L. Bayus (2001), "An Empirical Analysis of Firms' Product Line Decisions." *Journal of Marketing Research* 38 (February), 110–8.

Quelch, John A., and David Kenny (1994), "Extend Profits, Not Product Lines." *Harvard Business Review* (September–October), 153–60.

Raj, S. P. (1982), "The Effects of Advertising on High and Low Loyalty Consumer Segments." *Journal of Consumer Research* 9 (1) (June), 77–89.

Randall, Taylor, Karl Ulrich, and David Reibstein (1998), "Brand Equity and Vertical Product Line Extent." *Marketing Science* 17 (4), 356–79.

Rangaswamy, Arvind, Raymond R. Burke, and Terence A. Oliva (1993), "Brand Equity and the Extendibility of Brand Names." *International Journal of Research in Marketing,* 10 (1), 61–75.

Rao, Akshay R. (1997), "Strategic Brand Alliances." *The Journal of Brand Management* 5 (2), 111–9.

Rao, Akshay R., and Kent B. Monroe (1989), "The Effect of Price, Brand Name, and Store Name on Buyers' Perceptions of Product Quality: An Integrative Review." *Journal of Marketing Research* 26 (August), 351–7.

Rao, Akshay R., Lu Qu, and Robert W. Ruekert (1999), "Signaling Unobservable Product Quality Through a Brand Ally." *Journal of Marketing Research* 36 (May), 258–68.

Ratneshwar, S., David Glen Mick, and Cynthia Huffman, Eds. (2000), *The Why of Consumption: Contemporary Perspectives on Consumer Motives, Goals and Desires.* London, U.K.: Routledge.

Reddy, Srinivas K., Susan L. Holak, and Subodh Bhat (1994), "To Extend or Not to Extend: Success Determinants of Line Extensions." *Journal of Marketing Research* 31 (May), 243–62.

Richins, Marsha L. (1994), "Valuing Things: The Public and Private Meanings of Possessions." *Journal of Consumer Research* 21 (3) (December), 504–21.

Robertson, Kim R. (1989), "Strategically Desirable Brand Name Characteristics." *Journal of Consumer Marketing* 6 (4), 61–71.

Romeo, Jean B. (1991), "The Effect of Negative Information on the Evaluations of Brand Extensions and the Family Brand." In *Advances in Consumer Research* vol. 18, eds. Rebecca H. Holman and Michael R. Solomon, 399–406. Provo, Utah: Association for Consumer Research.

Russell, Gary J., and Wagner A. Kamakura (1994), "Understanding Brand Competition Using Micro and Macro Scanner Data." *Journal of Marketing Research* 31 (May), 289–303.

Samu, Sridhar, H. Shanker Krishnan, and Robert E. Smith (1999), "Using Advertising Alliances for New Product Introduction: Interactions Between Product Complementarity and Promotional Strategies." *Journal of Marketing* 63 (1) (January), 57–74.

Sappington, David E. M., and Birger Wernerfelt (1985), "To Brand or Not to Brand? A Theoretical and Empirical Question." *Journal of Business* 58 (3), 279–93.

Sawyer, A. G. (1981), "Repetition, Cognitive Response, and Persuasion." In *Cognitive Responses to Persuasion,* eds. R. Petty, T. Ostrum, and T. Brock, 237–262. Hillsdale, N.J.: Erlbaum.

Schmitt, Bernd H. (1997), "'Superficial out of Profundity': The Branding of Customer Experiences." *The Journal of Brand Management* 5 (2), 92–8.

Schmitt, Bernd H. (1999a), "Experiential Marketing." *Journal of Marketing Management* 15, 53–67.

Schmitt, Bernd H. (1999b), *Experiential Marketing: How to Get Customers to Sense, Feel, Think, Act, Relate to Your Company and Brands.* New York, N.Y.: Free Press.

Schmitt, Bernd H., and Laurette Dubé (1992), "Contextualized Representations of Brand Extensions: Are Feature Lists or Frames the Basic Components of Consumer Cognition?" *Marketing Letters* 3 (2), 115–26.

Schmitt, Bernd H., Yigang Pan, and Nader T. Tavassoli (1994), "Language and Consumer Memory: The Impact of Linguistic Differences between Chinese and English." *Journal of Consumer Research* 21 (12) (December), 419–31.

Schmitt, Bernd H., and Alex Simonson (1997), *Marketing Aesthetics: The Strategic Management of Brands, Identity and Image.* New York, N.Y.: Free Press.

Schouten, John W., and James H. McAlexander (1995), "Subcultures of Consumption: An Ethnography of the New Bikers." *Journal of Consumer Research* 22 (1) (June), 43–61.

Schumann, David W., J. M. Hathcote, and S. West (1991). "Corporate Advertising in America: A Review of Published Studies on Use, Measurement, and Effectiveness." *Journal of Advertising* 20 (September), 36–56.

Sen, Sankar (1999), "The Effects of Brand Name Suggestiveness and Decision Goal on the Development of Brand Knowledge." *Journal of Consumer Psychology* 8 (4), 431–55.

Sen, Sankar, and C. B. Bhattacharya (2001), "Does Doing Good Always Lead to Doing Better? Consumer Reactions to Corporate Social Responsibility." *Journal of Marketing Research* 38 (May), 225–43.

Sethuraman, Raj (1996), "A Model of How Discounting High-Priced Brands Affects the Sales of Low-Priced Brands." *Journal of Marketing Research* 33 (November), 399–409.

Sheinin, Daniel A. (1998), "Sub-brand Evaluation and Use versus Brand Extension." *The Journal of Brand Management* 6 (2), 113–22.

Shocker, Allan D., Rajendra K. Srivastava, and Robert W. Ruekert (1994), "Challenges and Opportunities Facing Brand Management: An Introduction to the Special Issue." *Journal of Marketing Research* 31 (May), 149–58.

Shugan, Steven M. (1989), "Branded Variants." In *Research in Marketing: AMA Educators' Proceedings Series #55,* eds. Paul Bloom et al. , 33–8. Chicago, Ill.: American Marketing Association.

Simon, Carol J., and Mary W. Sullivan (1993), "The Measurement and Determinants of Brand Equity: A Financial Approach." *Marketing Science* 12 (1) (Winter), 28–52.

Simon, Hermann (1979), "Dynamics of Price Elasticity and Brand Life Cycles: An Empirical Study." *Journal of Marketing Research* 16 (November), 439–52.

Simonin, Bernard L., and Julie A. Ruth (1998), "Is a Company Known by the Company It Keeps? Assessing the Spillover Effects of Brand Alliances on Consumer Brand Attitudes." *Journal of Marketing Research* 35 (February), 30–42.

Simonson, Alex F. (1995), "How and When Do Trademarks Dilute: A Behavioral Framework to Judge 'Likelihood' of Dilution." *The Trademark Reporter* 83, 149–74.

Simonson, Itamar (1994), "Trademark Infringement from the Buyer Perspective: Conceptual Analysis and Measurement Implications." *Journal of Public Policy and Marketing* 13 (2), 181–99.

Simonson, Itamar, Joel Huber, and John Payne (1988), "The Relationship Between Prior Brand Knowledge and Information Acquisition Order." *Journal of Consumer Research* 14 (March), 566–78.

Sivakumar K., and S. P. Raj (1997), "Quality Tier Competition: How Price Change Influences Brand Choice and Category Choice." *Journal of Marketing* 61 (3) (July), 71–84.

Smith, Daniel C. (1992), "Brand Extensions and Advertising Efficiency: What Can and Cannot Be Expected." *Journal of Advertising Research* (November/December), 11–20.

Smith, Daniel C., and Jonlee Andrews (1995), "Rethinking the Effect of Perceived Fit on Customers' Evaluations of New Products." *Journal of the Academy of Marketing Science* 23 (1) (Winter), 4–14.

Smith, Daniel C., and C. Whan Park (1992), "The Effects of Brand Extensions on Market Share and Advertising Efficiency." *Journal of Marketing Research* 29 (August), 296–313.

Smith, Robert E. (1993), "Integrating Information from Advertising and Trial: Processes and Effects on Consumer Response to Product Information." *Journal of Marketing Research* 30 (May), 204–19.

Solomon, Michael R., and Basil G. Englis (1992), "Consumption Constellations: Implications for Integrated Marketing Communications." In *Integrated Marketing Communications,* eds. Jeri Moore and Esther Thorson, 65–86. Hillsdale, N.J.: Erlbaum.

Srinivasan, V. (1979), "Network Models for Estimating Brand-Specific Effects in Multi-Attribute Marketing Models." *Management Science* 25 (1), 11–21.

Srivastava, Rajendra K., Tasadduq A. Shervani, and Liam Fahey (1998), "Market-Based Assets and Shareholder Value." *Journal of Marketing* 62 (1) (January), 2–18.

Sternthal, Brian, and C. S. Craig (1984), *Consumer Behavior: An Information Processing Perspective.* Englewood Cliffs, N.J.: Prentice Hall.

Stewart, David W., and David H. Furse (1986), *Effective Television Advertising: A Study of 1000 Commercials.* Lexington, Mass.: Lexington Books.

Sullivan, Mary W. (1990), "Measuring Image Spillovers in Umbrella-Branded Products." *The Journal of Business* 63 (3), 309–29.

Sullivan, Mary W. (1992), "Brand Extensions: When to Use Them." *Management Science* 38 (6), 793–806.

Sullivan, Mary W. (1998), "How Brand Names Affect the Demand for Twin Automobiles." *Journal of Marketing Research* 35 (5), 154–65.

Sullivan, Mary W. (2001), "How Many Trademarks Does It Take to Protect a Brand? The Optimal Number of Trademarks, Branding Strategy, and Brand Performance." Washington, D. C.: U.S. Department of Justice, Working Paper.

Swait, Joffre, Tülin Erdem, Jordan Louviere, and Chris Dubelaar (1993), "The Equalization Price: A Measure of Consumer-Perceived Brand Equity." *International Journal of Research in Marketing* 10 (1) (March), 23–45.

Swaminathan, Vanitha, Richard J. Fox, and Srinivas K. Reddy (2001), "The Impact of Brand Extension Introduction on Choice." *Journal of Marketing* 65 (4) (October), 1–15.

Teas, R. Kenneth, and Terry H. Grapentine (1996). "Demystifying Brand Equity." *Marketing Research* 8 (2), 25–9.

Tellis, Gerard J., and Peter N. Golder (1996), "First to Market, First to Fail? Real Causes of Enduring Market Leadership." *Sloan Management Review* 37 (2), 65–75.

Thakor, Mrugank V., and Barney G. Pacheco (1997), "Foreign Branding and Its Effects on Product Perceptions and Attitudes: A Replication and Extension in a Multicultural Setting." *Journal of Marketing Theory and Practice* (Winter), 15–30.

Van Osselaer, Stijn M. J., and Joseph W. Alba (2000), "Consumer Learning and Brand Equity." *Journal of Consumer Research* 27 (June), 1–16.

Van Osselaer, Stijn M. J., and Chris Janiszewski (2001), "Two Ways of Learning Brand Associations." *Journal of Consumer Research* 28 (2) (September), 202–23.

Vanden Bergh, Bruce G., Keith Adler, and Lauren Oliver (1987), "Linguistic Distinction among Top Brand Names." *Journal of Advertising Research* (August/September), 39–44.

Vanden Bergh, Bruce G., J. Collins, M. Schultz, and Keith Adler (1984), "Sound Advice on Brand Names." *Journalism Quarterly* 61 (4), 835–40.

Varadarajan, P. Rajan, and Anil Menon (1988), "Cause-Related Marketing: A Coalignment of Marketing Strategy and Corporate Philanthropy." *Journal of Marketing* 52 (July), 58–74.

Venkatesh, R., and Vijay Mahajan (1997), "Products with Branded Components: An Approach for Premium Pricing and Partner Selection." *Marketing Science* 16 (2), 146–65.

Voss, Kevin E., and P. Tansuhaj (1999), "A Consumer Perspective on Foreign Market Entry: Building Brands Through Brand Alliances." *Journal of International Consumer Marketing* 11 (2), 39–58.

Wänke, M., Herman Bless, and Norbert Schwarz (1998), "Context Effects in Product Line Extensions: Context Is Not Destiny." *Journal of Consumer Psychology* 7 (4), 299–322.

Weinburger, Mark G., and C. Gulas (1992), "The Impact of Humor in Advertising: A Review." *Journal of Advertising* 21 (4), 35–60.

Wernerfelt, Birger (1988), "Umbrella Branding as a Signal of New Product Quality: An Example of Signaling by Posting a Bond." *Rand Journal of Economics* 19 (3), 458–66.

Yoo, Boonghee, Naveen Donthu, and Sungho Lee (2000), "An Examination of Selected Marketing Mix Elements and Brand Equity." *Journal of the Academy of Marketing Science* 28 (2) (Spring), 195–211.

Yorkston, Eric A. (2000), "Construction Through Deconstruction: A Compositional Approach to the Development of Brand Names." New York, N.Y.: New York University, Ph.D. Dissertation.

Yorkston, Eric A., and G. Menon (2001), "A Sound Idea: Phonetic Effects of Brand Names on Consumer Judgments." Los Angeles, Calif.: University of Southern California, Marshall School of Business, Working Paper.

Zaichkowsky, Judith (1995), *Defending Your Brand Against Imitation.* Westpoint, Colo.: Quorom Books.

Zaltman, Gerald, and Robin H. Coulter (1995), "Seeing the Voice of the Consumer: Metaphor-based Advertising Research." *Journal of Advertising Research* 35 (4), 35–51.

Zaltman, Gerald, and Robin A. Higie (1993), "Seeing the Voice of the Customer: The Zaltman Metaphor Elicitation Technique." Cambridge, Mass.: Marketing Science Institute, Report 93–114.

Zhang, Shi, and Bernd H. Schmitt (2001), "Creating Local Brands in Multilingual International Markets." *Journal of Marketing Research* 38 (August), 313–25.

Zhang, Shi, and Sanjay Sood (2002), "'Deep' and 'Surface' Cues: Brand Extension Evaluations by Children and Adults." *Journal of Consumer Research* 29 (June), 129–141.

Zinkhan, George M., and Claude R. Martin, Jr. (1987), "New Brand Names and Inferential Beliefs: Some Insights on Naming New Products." *Journal of Business Research* 15 (2), 157–72.

ABOUT THE AUTHOR

Kevin Lane Keller is the E. B. Osborn Professor of Marketing at the Amos Tuck School of Business Administration at Dartmouth College. Professor Keller received his B.A. in mathematics and economics from Cornell University in 1978, his MBA from Carnegie-Mellon University's Graduate School of Industrial Administration in 1980, and his Ph.D. in marketing from Duke University's Fuqua School of Business in 1986.

Previously, Professor Keller was on the faculty of the Graduate School of Business at Stanford University, where he also served as the head of the marketing group. Additionally, he has been on the marketing faculty of the Schools of Business Administration at the University of California at Berkeley and the University of North Carolina at Chapel Hill, has been a Visiting Professor at Duke University and the Australian Graduate School of Management, and has two years of industry experience as marketing consultant for Bank of America.

Professor Keller's general area of expertise lies in consumer marketing. His specific research interest is in how understanding theories and concepts related to consumer behavior can improve advertising and branding strategies. His advertising and branding research has been published in the *Journal of Marketing, Journal of Marketing Research,* and *Journal of Consumer Research*. He also sits on the Editorial Review Boards of those journals and is an Academic Trustee of the Marketing Science Institute. With over thirty published papers, his research has been widely cited and has received numerous awards. He is also the author of a textbook, *Strategic Brand Management,* whose second edition was published in August 2002 by Prentice Hall.

ABOUT MSI

The Marketing Science Institute connects business people and academic researchers who are committed to advancing marketing in order to achieve higher levels of business performance. Founded in 1961, MSI currently brings together executives from approximately 70 sponsoring corporations with leading researchers from over 100 universities worldwide.

As a nonprofit institution, MSI financially supports academic research for the development—and practical translation—of leading-edge marketing knowledge on topics of importance to business. Issues of key importance to business performance are identified by the Board of Trustees, which represents MSI corporations and the academic community. MSI supports studies by academics on these issues and disseminates the results through conferences and workshops, as well as through its publications series.

Related MSI Working Papers

93-126 "How Expansion Advertising Affects Brand Usage Frequency: A Programmatic Evaluation" by Brian Wansink and Michael L. Ray

93-124 "An Approach to Assess the Importance of Brand Equity in Acquisition Decisions" by Vijay Mahajan, Rajendra K. Srivastava, and Vithala R. Rao

93-120 "Using Dominance Measures to Evaluate Brand Extensions" by Paul M. Herr, Peter H. Farquhar, and Russell H. Fazio

93-101 "New Tools for Understanding Brand Competition: Integrating Household and Retail Scanner Data" by Gary J. Russell and Wagner A. Kamakura

92-133 "The Long-term Differentiation Value of Marketing Communication Actions" by William Boulding, Eunkyu Lee, and Richard Staelin

92-131 "Market Value of Trademarks Measured via Trademark Litigation" by Sanjai Bhagat and U. N. Umesh

92-129 "Retail Power: Monster or Mouse?" by Paul W. Farris and Kusum L. Ailawadi

92-128 "The Effect of Marketplace Factors on Private Label Penetration in Grocery Products" by Raj Sethuraman

92-123 "A Schema Unification Model of Brand Extensions" by Sheri Bridges

92-122 "Diluting Beliefs about Family Brands: When Brand Extensions Have a Negative Impact" by Deborah Roedder John and Barbara Loken

92-116 "A Financial Approach to Estimating Firm-Level Brand Equity and Measuring the Impact of Marketing Events" by Carol J. Simon and Mary Sullivan

92-105 "Promotion Has a Negative Effect on Brand Evaluations—Or Does It? Additional Disconfirming Evidence" by Scott Davis, Jeffrey Inman, and Leigh McAlister

91-130 "Price and Brand Name as Indicators of Quality Dimensions" by Merrie Brucks and Valarie A. Zeithaml

91-124 "Brand Equity: A Perspective on Its Meaning and Measurement" by Rajendra K. Srivastava and Allan D. Shocker